BEING THE MIRACLE OF LOVE

ALSO BY
HOPE IVES MAURAN

AVAILABLE IN PRINT
*Where the Wisdom Lies: A Message From Nature's
Small Creatures (2006)*

AVAILABLE IN PRINT, eBOOK AND MP3 RECORDING
*Be The Second Coming: Guidebook to the Embodiment
of the Christ Within: A Personal Journey,
Our Collective Destiny (2011)*

TEACHING AUDIO CD: WRITTEN AND RECORDED
*Emotional Transformation: Learn to Speak the
Language of Creation (2005)*

BEING THE MIRACLE OF LOVE

Conversations With Jesus...

HOPE IVES MAURAN

Legwork Team Publishing
New York

Legwork Team Publishing
www.legworkteam.com
Phone: 631-944-6511

Copyright © 2013 Hope Ives Mauran

ISBN: 978-1-935905-58-5 (sc)
ISBN: 978-1-935905-60-8 (e)

First Edition 08/02/2013

Printed in the United States of America
This book is printed on acid-free paper

Book Design by Gayle L. Newman
Cover Illustration and Design by Michael Stack of
Mebu Design & Marketing

Love is the healing elixir of life.
It is a physical substance
at both the human level and the Divine level
and it is the glue, the back ground music
and substrate of existence.

—Jesus Chapter 7

ABOUT
THE COVER:

As I lay in Shavasana, the corpse pose during a recent yoga class, a peaceful, strong energy descended upon me. I had a vision for the cover of this book of a human light body, standing in a lotus blossom, in a tube of white light, inside of an egg shaped structure. At the time, it seemed beautiful and mysterious. I realize only now, as the book is going off to print, that this is a continuation of a painting that I did a few years ago entitled *'Transformation.'*

'Transformation' illustrates the process of awakening, cleansing and rebirth that is often part of the spiritual journey. The painting is done on three canvases, one above the next. Using the same photograph in different sizes, the woman in the bottom frame is asleep in the sunshine amidst the density of the world. Like most of us, she sleeps through life, unaware that there is a greater reality and magnificent possibility inherent within human life. As her world breaks apart she awakens and is uplifted and tossed as she moves towards the lily stem. In the middle frame, she moves upward through the stem, first as it is growing through the muck and then through the cleansing water. In awakening in this way, she has shed her ideas about life, her limitations and her beliefs that held her from knowing herself as the creator God that she is. In the top frame she rises to stand naked, reborn in the center of the lily flower, in an unfamiliar, Light world. Naked is used as a metaphor to mean that, she has shed the false ideas

about herself: both limiting and inflated, and is available to be the eyes, ears, hands and feet of her Higher Self.

The cover art for this book, beautifully rendered by Michael Stack of Mebu Design & Marketing, takes this journey to the next step, where the human who is cleansed of human consciousness is filled with Light. The Antahkarana, or the tube of Christ Light, that connects us to our Christed Self and beyond that to the God Head, descends through the crown of the head to the heart and the body is filled with Light... *"the full fusion of the Spiritual Light Of God with the flesh of the human form, creates an Ascension body."* This transformation is preceded by a grand shift in consciousness: from human consciousness to God Consciousness. In chapter 5, Jesus describes Ascension and the process of allowing the God Self to inhabit the body and says that this is the destiny of all humans. This is the future that awaits us all.

Jesus reassuringly offers this... *'And so Dear Ones, be not daunted by this task, be ever ready to surrender to the divine Grace of your Higher Being and know that as the body you inhabit evolves in its God Consciousness, this opportunity will come closer and closer.'* (pg. 52)

Transformation
Mixed Media, (3)18x18 canvases
View it in color at
www.hopeivesmauran.com

Photo credit: Maggie Heinzel-Neel

Jesus: *I dedicate this book to those*
who come in the guise of human form,
and transcend the limitation of that definition,
to embody their fullness as the Christ,
and to those such as you who read these words.

Hope: I dedicate this book to spiritual master
Her Holiness Sai Maa Lakshmi Devi,
whose Love inspires and guides us
to our own Mastery and embodiment as Love.

MY DEEPEST GRATITUDE AND APPRECIATION TO:

Elise, Rall and **James,** for family in the finest sense: supportive, enthusiastic and unconditionally loving. **Hetty Rodenburg**, author of *Dreaming a Lighthouse*, for the quote from Jesus, **Jai Shree Devi,** of Her Holiness Sai Maa's office, for reviewing the manuscript's parts that mention Sai Maa. **Jody Fabrikant**, amazing, patient and persistent editor and insightful and generous friend—who jokingly gave the book the sub title: *A Return To Grace in A world Beyond Grammar*! It has been a joy working together. **Lester England**, an inspiring and uplifting reminder of who I Am, who speaks as ONE through his Human voice, a rare and precious gift. Les' quote and two Big Questions grace this book. **Maria Gabriella Molnar**, dear friend, honest editor and the one who brought the blessing of Sai Maa into my life. **Michael Ebeling of Ebeling & Associates Literary Agency**, thanks for your vision, energy and encouragement. **Michael Schwaebe**, treasured friend and healer. **Michael Stack of Mebu Designs & Marketing,** for creating the amazing cover design, I have felt the hand of the Divine in our every interaction. **Mom and Dad**, for the gifts of life, love and abundance consciousness. **Richard Iadarola**, healer, editor, networker, light message facilitator and uplifting friend, (who also stars in the first chapter...). **Craig Hamilton,**

for the Principles of Evolutionary Culture[1] and for being a role model of the embodied presence of Love. **Raymon Grace**, for the amazing tools of empowerment that you share so freely and for promptly and generously responding to my inquiries. **Roy Capellaro,** for Love, tea and miracles. **Tom Deile**, dear friend who offered to hold my hat in Chapter 4.

A huge thank you to **Yvonne Kamerling and Janet Yudewitz of Legwork Team Publishing**. Our gratitude to them and their team of design, editorial and technical professionals for transforming the manuscript into the book you hold in your hands.

There is One Life, One Body and One Mind... no part of the One is separable. Thank you to all who are a part of this Life, I am so grateful for your friendship and for sharing this journey with you.

---

1   The Principles of Evolutionary Culture are available on this web page: http://www.integralenlightenment.com/pages/articles/index. php?id=763899701

CONTENTS

Jesus or Jeshua's words are in *italics*.

Capitalized words like Source, Self, Love, Divine and Life refer to the divinized Christed or unified Higher Octave of the word that is capitalized. There is a glossary of terms in the back of the book.

LIST OF EXERCISES

This book invites your own self-inquiry. There are places in the text where simple exercises and practices are offered. You may wish to take the time and do these practices. It is in the practice of living this, not just knowing it, that we are transformed. In reading the words in this book through the eyes of our Higher Self or our Christed Self, these words will create potential and coherency within us and perhaps quiet our doubting mind.

'AUTHOR'S' NOTE

In 2009, I was asked by Spirit to write *A Guidebook To Christ Consciousness.'* I wondered how I could write such a book, until thankfully I remembered that I could communicate internally with anyone, so why not ask Jesus... an expert on Christ Consciousness! At the time, I didn't realize that 'Christ' is a word that means 'one who embodies God' and that each of us has the potential to make that free will choice to do so. That book was published in 2011 under the name *Be The Second Coming.*

This book that you hold right now, the second in the series, is the result of my continued conversations with Jesus. When I was asked to write this book on the topic of the new Golden Age, I realized that I had no idea what a new Golden Age might be like here on Earth. How could I imagine a new world when I only had the present world to work from? I now realize that the new world will *result* from a human population that is living from Unity or Christ Consciousness, which practically speaking, means living *as, from* and *in* Love. The choice to live from Love is present already for each of us in our every interaction.

My life and 'who I know myself to be' have been transformed by communicating with Jesus and by practicing the things he teaches. My hope is that His message will find in you a willing ear, for it has the potential to transform you and your life too. That may seem obvious, but prior to communicating with Jesus directly, I was not very open to hearing about him or his message, so I guess I really shouldn't have been surprised by how Jesus' name in the first book made the book inaccessible to many people. So I asked... "Jesus, there are people who resist your name, even the mention of it and I wonder if there is anything that you could say that would help them to be open to your message?"

Dear One, this is a question that has plagued me for generation after generation. My name and my Life have been both desecrated and molded to fit unclean motives and distortion of my True message. The real reason that life is not what it should be on the Earth is because of the ulterior motives of the many who have isolated the masses by holding my word over them! There is nothing farther from my wish and desire and I appreciate your question—not one too many have asked! It would seem that simply sharing your message and allowing the Truth to reveal itself to each individual in their own timing is what is possible. Rigidity in any form is like the wall to a jail and it is exceedingly discomforting to me that my name is used to further such isolation among people.

Grace and Love are my messages; empowerment and harmony are my gifts. Each will choose as they are ready. That is all I can say!

So here you have *Being The Miracle Of Love:* a blueprint of the Golden Age and further insights and practices to assist you to embody Love's higher potential, which is available to you right now.

JESUS' INTRODUCTION

Greetings Dear Ones, thank you for joining me in these pages of Light, for there is a great transformation occurring now on Earth and this work is deeply connected with the future of Life on Planet Earth. What is needed now on Earth is vision, vision to assist the creative faculty of the human species to enlist the Higher Realms in its thoughts of what will happen. What is being created on the threshold of this New World is coming from the hearts and minds of those who envision it and also from those who don't. The unconscious human is a recording and playback device, the human creates by thoughts that often dwell upon things 'as they are,' so more of 'what already is' is thus created. The human doesn't realize this, thinking that the happenings of life are beyond his control.

The future is felt in many ways on Earth, one way is as though it is cast in stone, another way is that it is of our own making, we would like to say it is both—both in the same way it is the creation and the evolution, both in the way it is the chicken and the egg. You see, the vibration of the Earth is rising and that is a change that is set in stone; the human faculty of thought now creates even more powerfully as this occurs. As Humanity realizes their power to create the world, the Earth will change. As these two forces harmonize, there is a chance for creation as it is meant to be: unified within the heart and mind of the human and embraced within the concept and paradigm of God, which is beneficent, all powerful and fulfilling for the human race to embark in partnership with. So what this book might offer you and your children's children, is the chance for a life of joy, abundance and Truth.

And so Dear Ones Welcome! Welcome to the place where the Truth of what is present right here right now may be revealed and thus the key to what will bring a New World into being is made manifest.

I bring to you now the words through the vessel Hope, that she might assist our work into the world at levels that were not available without her surrender to this process. This process for her is like 'she' is writing the book, when in truth the Higher Self of Hope, in tandem with the Christed being Jesus is writing this book. In the grace of that partnership, that Unity, that Love, these words come forth for your perusal, your contemplation and your practice.

Much of this book is on the concept of Unity within the many—e pluribus unum²—a way of being on the Earth that brings Earth to the next level of Light and Love and Harmony. So within this mandate for union within diversity, the details of life need to be hammered out. The details of a new way of living on Earth are required so that the new Earth may reveal itself to you and through you. It is not set in detailed destiny, it is set in grand strokes, waiting for the details by your vision and Love and Grace to be revealed through your thoughts, your choices, your efforts and non-efforts.

---

2   'e pluribus unum' is Latin and translates to : 'out of many, one.'

You see, the human race is a powerful force, one that can make or break the natural systems on Earth at this time. So the real choice for each and every one who finds themselves incarnated on planet Earth at this delicious time, is to find the will to enact the True Self in life; to find the self-awareness and the present moment often enough to reveal the Love that you are to the world. Through each individual, within each interaction, the New World is born. And so this work that you now hold is a handbook to that creative adventure.

The task might be overwhelming except for one thing: it is the reality that the Christ Mind, the God That You Are is present within you and all you need do to reveal this is allow it. It may be the human tendency to deprecate the self and think on those areas of lack or concern within the life you lead, areas that may not be 'up to the task' of creating the structures and relationships of the new Golden Age. This is ok, for those aspects of yourself that are your true nature are already within you, available to your life by your willingness and your comfort in surrender. And so Dear One, relax, put your feet up, settle back in a cozy spot and read on, for the future that is being created wishes for you to take this in with an open heart so that it might become a reference to the planners of the New World.

We will illustrate the New World into reality within your mind and thus it's blueprints will be made real. This is the true nature of information such as this; it is a blueprint, that by your thoughts upon it, by fleshing it out into your life, you become the architect of the New World. And the life that you lead then creates the new opportunity that exists right now on Earth. So enjoy our time together, we are as aware of your reading this as you are. There is only One, We Are One and as such the unity of all is formulated through each of us, aligned to true Heart, Mind, Spirit and Authority. With Love and Grace I welcome you.

Your beloved, honored friend and brother, Jesus

1. AN AGE OF MIRACLES

I was in line waiting to get into the hall to see Sai Maa Lakshmi Devi, an enlightened master and a jagadguru in a 5000 year lineage of gurus, when a man came up to me and said… "Don't I know you from somewhere?" I didn't recognize him. We began talking and as it turned out we had many common interests and shared references. His name was Richard and we ended up sitting together towards the front of the hall. It was the month after I had taken Sai Maa's Journey of Profound Healing, which was just that, a journey and profound and it left me changed in a way that I had been powerless to enact for myself. My heart was more open to Life and little did I know that in coming to see her again, I would experience two more miracles.

As we waited for Sai Maa to arrive, Richard asked me what I did. I had just gotten a copy of my first book, *Be The Second Coming* from the printer, so I pulled the book out of my bag and showed it to him. He took it and held it to his chest and closed his eyes, evidently sensing the book's energy and then he flipped through it, reading a line here and there. He gave it back to me and pronounced it "awesome." It was the first time I had shared the book with a stranger and I was pleased to have him accept it in such a unique way, it touched my heart.

Sai Maa guided us through an energy exercise where we placed our hands in front of us and felt the energy between them. As we focused upon the energy, we created a ball of energy that became more and more tangible. She suggested we infuse it with something so I put Jesus into mine. We were then directed to put the ball of energy into our bodies somewhere and I put mine into my heart. I felt a wave of energy pour through me. A short while later, I had the experience that I was no longer inside of me, but instead inside of Richard, I was Richard. I was inside of him and it was as natural as being inside of 'me,' it felt intimate and familiar, I felt at home. Suddenly, I felt uncomfortable and quickly withdrew in the way one might from leaning on a stranger's door when it unexpectedly pops open. I didn't tell Richard what had happened, feeling a social boundary had been breached. Nonetheless I was filled with wonder afterwards at the union I felt with an almost total stranger and the experience of being him. Being inside of him in that moment, in that way, was like a peek through Christ's eyes, that was miracle number one.

A day later, Richard and I met again and I confessed that I had the experience of *being him* and how wonderful it felt to experience such tangible oneness. He of course had no idea it had happened. I shared with him my wonderment that it was *even possible* to be inside of someone else like that.

He said he wanted to talk with me, so we arranged to have breakfast together before the next day's program. A large potential of some sort loomed over that meeting and as I sat with him out on the terrace in the morning sunshine, he talked. He said he wanted me to answer some questions. He said "Put your hand over your heart and see how you feel when you say 'I lived in Israel.'" I repeated "I lived in Israel" I felt no misalignment. Then he said and I repeated "I lived in the time of Jesus." I had never thought of such a thing... I felt aligned. And then he said "I hung out with Jesus." With each question, an opening expanded within me. When I repeated his statement "I hung out with Jesus." I burst into tears for a few seconds at the realization that it was true. Well, *that* had never occurred to me! The very real feeling in my heart helped me to realize that this idea was true that I actually knew Jesus when he was on Earth! So I share this with you to convey the openness and the joy that resulted from that exchange with Richard. I was joyfully reunited inside me with something that I had been separate from and was now able to receive and express; I felt a greater clarity of purpose.

It shed some light on the non-religious path that had brought me to this focus upon Jesus and Christ consciousness. My only previous interactions with Jesus or his teachings have been through recent first hand encounters, so putting my relationship with him into a past life framework made sense because nothing in my current life or upbringing would have pointed me in this direction.[3] It would make sense if one were previously a follower of Jesus' teachings to write a book on the embodiment of Christ consciousness. So the realization I had as a result of my conversation with Richard put something in a much greater

---

3   Two of my encounters with Jesus are recounted in *Be The Second Coming*, one with an illustration.

perspective and I was very grateful to him for having the vision and courage to walk me to that realization. In retrospect Richard's initial question to me "don't I know you from somewhere" was right on the mark, just a few lifetimes late!

After that experience, I was in Love with life and with everyone around me; it was as though something that had held me from being open was pierced like a bubble! We went back into the ballroom and I was feeling Love in a way that I had *never* felt it before. Love was an actual substance that literally filled my body from my feet to my head, my body felt very different.

Sai Maa creates an energy field where people repeatedly speak of their hearts being opened in her presence. Later as Sai Maa was walking in the aisles of the hall talking to people, she noticed me and said… "tell me something Hope." I said "I am filled with Love… Thank you." She said "Yes, I can see it in your aura." The Second Miracle happened shortly thereafter—on the way to the rest room!

The large hall had been transformed into a sacred space for the gathering of 800 people and the energy was very high. I slipped out of the aisle past Richard and walked purposefully toward the double doors to go to the rest room. Since the program was still in session, I thought to open the door quietly. In that instant, the door smoothly glided open in choreographed perfection for me to walk through. I was delighted for the synchronicity and was ready to say 'thank you, that was perfect timing' to the person on the other side of the door. I looked backwards and the space where someone should have been standing was empty, no one was there! The door had opened 'on its own.' There was one person in the outer lobby and I remarked to her with delight… "that door just opened by itself, no one's there!" We both stood there and stared at the empty space for a moment and then I continued on down the hall.

I glowed after the miracle of the door opening, it was so unexpected. But when my mind tried to explain it, there was only emptiness—which perhaps elucidated the gap between the mind's pattern of knowing and an experience out of its reach. Perhaps miracles happen in a realm that the small separate self cannot enter! Maybe the world that exists full of miracles is right here now, and we just don't know it.

And then I simply carried on with life as though it was the same as before. Yet the proof that miracles are possible was now undeniable. Having made such claims through Jesus' words in *Be The Second Coming*, I was absolved of that remaining doubt I held about miracles. That doubt was the stepchild of generations of doors that required opening by human effort!

Much later I wondered *how* it had happened, what exactly is required for such a miracle to occur? Of course the wild card in that experience was the grace, energy and presence of Her Holiness Sai Maa Lakshmi Devi, her many students and the energy of Jesus that I had placed into myself. But being new to her circle of influence, I wasn't aware that she was 'behind' the opening door, I have subsequently heard others mention doors miraculously opening! I now realize that the way in which I was joined with Richard, she is joined with me. She embodies Divine Love, perhaps the same higher octave of Love that filled me so completely that day. In that Love and by the Presence that Sai

Maa embodies, she shows us all what is possible.

It's easy to write off miracles as the stuff of fairy tales, but not when they happen to one directly! Miracles such as these will be commonplace in the Golden Age. This book will perhaps reveal some of the higher possibilities and new potentials for life on Earth that result from our remembrance of our identity as Love and our willingness to step through doors within ourselves. I share these stories with you of a 'door' opening inward and a door opening outward, to illustrate the frontier that is available to us all right here now. The doors to the Golden Age are open... Welcome!

2. LOVE AND PERFECTION

There is a passage in the book that I read this morning called *'Love Without End, Jesus Speaks'* by Glenda Green, that feels like the perfect explanation of the miracles in Denver. *"The heart, in its perfection is the one connection with your Creator which was never severed. But it must regain its certainty over illusion! All miracles happen that way. The heart is the bringer of all miracles."*[4]

"The heart is the bringer of all miracles" a phrase that sits with me now. The actual experience of Love in advance of the door opening was a dense fullness that was like food, it literally filled me. I wasn't hungry; I was 'full' with Love, Christ Love. The Love was not local to my heart; it was a whole body experience, I *was* Love. It was like I *was* a miracle of love.

> *"Thing about Love is... it's not a thing but a who."*
>
> —cell phone text from my friend Les

4   Green, Glenda. *Love Without End, Jesus Speaks,* Sedona AZ, Spiritis, 1999. (pg. 56)

My curiosity was awakened, what would it take to *live* in that state of Love and certainty? What would it take to *be* like that? Sai Maa has said "Love is *who* you are" and "You *are* Love." What she means is that we actually *are* that Love, we just cover it up, hide it, deny it and bury it by our attitudes, beliefs, experiences, perspective, unconscious programming and expectations of who we think we are and how we view life.

A year after the miracles in Denver, I experienced that same full body Love, again in Sai Maa's presence, this time in Montreal. My youngest son was there with me and during one of the sessions, he fell asleep on my shoulder, a sweet moment that opened my heart and rendered me to stillness and 'non-doing' as he slept on and on, long after the session ended and the hall was empty. I finally stopped long enough to observe myself and was willing to ask: What is it that I 'do' to get in the way of this Love that is within me? If this is really my true nature and available to me *all the time*, in what way do I interfere with it so that my life is not simply one long Love affair?

Remembering the miracle of being able to ask Jesus questions… I asked "How can I cultivate a life *filled* with Love and Miracles?"

"Dear One, note that when these events occurred there was nothing standing between you and life, there were no obligations or needs of the moment or of the physical world. You were fully present, aligned to the true nature of your being, which is Love. The other thing you might wish to be aware of is the certainty with which you held yourself in those moments, you weren't in question about life, about anything, you were simply and only Love. This condition is conducive to miracles and the energy of

Life flowing within your realm of influence.

It is like this: imagine that you are a paper airplane and that you sail along on the winds. There is little you as the airplane need do, other than just 'be,' be still in being an airplane so that the environment around you might keep you aloft. You simply remain still as the motion of life around you furthers your journey. Not unlike the miracle of the opening door, you held yourself simply as Love and were carried aloft by the energy of Life. Your nano second of innocent desire to open the door without sound enabled such an occurrence. Realize the truth that you are 'that which made the door open' as much as you are 'the door' and 'the human body.' It is from this quite logical perspective that the door will open for you at this moment in time. For it is 'you,' the energy of the action that made it move is 'you' and the 'you' that set the desire in motion is 'you' as well. In the ease and alignment of 'being the Love that you are' or were at that moment, something beautiful occurred: a miracle.

It's not really anything beyond the ordinary in the world that the human family has inhabited thus far; it is simply now a time of revealing this world to those humans that are available to it. So no need for awe and speechless wonder at this 'miracle,' simply reveal to yourself the 'Love that you are' by staying out of its way and something really wondrous will peel back in your life. You will find that the

It may be helpful to look upon the world that surrounds you from the perspective of this universal Self, this 'One' for indeed it all makes sense if one can do this.

world is almost tripping over itself to serve your needs, simply because it is taking care of 'itself' as 'You.' You claim your True identity and nature—and the universe or 'All That Is' is then available through you to endear itself to the very ground upon which it walks as 'You.'

It may be helpful to look upon the world that surrounds you from the perspective of this universal Self, this 'One' for indeed it all makes sense if one can do this. It may be a manipulation, but it is a worthwhile one to enable you to relieve yourself of the tension on the isolated self that you have lived within for so long and allow the ease and relaxation of the Unified 'Self that you truly are' to inhabit your being. This would mean to be still enough within yourself to allow the whole Self, the 'Self in union with All That Is' to inhabit the body that you have called 'your own.' It is your choice to make this greater Self your true identity and that is why this condition of miracles is not one that everyone experiences.

The age of Light that is approaching is a time on Earth where this will become easier and more common. It is for this reason that this book is offered... to pave the way to a New World by revealing the future potential for Life on Earth. As you celebrate the coming of the new times and hold this higher potential as already yours, the way will simply reveal itself. There is no need to make this hard or distant; simply surrender to Love. The Love that you are and always have been, will reveal itself to you as you move through life not wishing for something other than what is revealed in front of you, simply being the presence of the Christed Self as the world unfolds around you.

These words... *"simply being the presence of the Christ Self as the world unfolds around you*" may be a bit daunting to the reader; can you explain that please so that it doesn't sound so unattainable?

Yes of course. The Christed Self is simply that aspect of 'who you are' that is present when the 'rest of who you are' is not interfering. The 'rest of who you are' is the (human) self that you have called yourself all these years of life: the wounds, the patterns, the proclivities, the surrendered powers to others, the wishes, the dreams, the hopes, the foibles, the unique aspects that make you 'You.' Now this doesn't mean you become a cardboard cutout of you, uninteresting and without expression. It means that the parts of you that don't serve this greater definition of yourself as 'the God force in action through your unique body vehicle,' those parts are let go of and the uniquely wondrous Self that remains is the Christ Self.

You see, as a human you are simply an expression of the One God. You are the One God in your unique vehicle. So using a car metaphor, as you remove the booties hanging from the rear view mirror and the scratch down the right side from that old altercation with a branch and the other things that make your car different, the essence of the car, the motor and the frame that holds it all, is the pure part one calls a 'car.' So your car is no different than the other cars in its essence, it is simply unique by how you have made it unique to you. Stripping the car (the self) of its excess expressions of 'you' enables another opportunity to reveal its (True) Self. This is where the car metaphor fails, but say the car once stripped could then fly through the air because it was lighter. This too you can do! What if the car could create instantly all the fuel and fluids it required? This too you can do! So it

11

> 'No one further from the Source than I Jesus.' That is the key; for it is the place from which all human endeavor of the highest order is possible.

is by becoming the essence and Truth of 'who you are beneath the clutter of past energetic and personality traits,' that something grandly universal and uniquely you is revealed.

It is already there, so don't go looking for it, you won't find it anywhere! Let your SELF free of yourself and the world will become a new place for you. This book, this hand book is for this very reason, a way of showing you the way to this revealing. Enjoy the journey to your SELF, to Love. It is the place to be! Nowhere else will bring you the joy and the wonder for Life that you are seeking in all the 'other' things you quest for in life. Fasten your seatbelt, we will be taking off shortly.

Thank you for this! I love you.

A Vision Of The New Earth

The Golden Age is a result of our *inner* transformation. We must begin *within* at the level of our beliefs about ourselves and Life to transform the outer world. I wonder if having a vision of the New Earth might make it easier to imagine the Earth in a state beyond living from the ego driven self and fear? Will you speak about what the New Earth might look or feel like?

Dear One, No one further from the source than I, No one not healed of all discord internally, No one aligned to the structural physical world. These paradigms of a changed reality are what awaits

the human family. 'No one further from the Source than I Jesus.'
That is the key; for it is the place from which all human endeavor
of the highest order is possible. You see, the human creates from
the platform they build for themselves. If they live on the platform
of victim hood and non-responsibility for self (through thoughts
and other expressions), then there is a level of life that is lived
that must include experiences of victim hood.[5] *If on the other end*
of the spectrum, a human lives knowing they are 'no further from
the source than I, Jesus,' then they have a mature perspective,
they are responsible to themselves and 'All That Is' and they hold
the Truth of Unity and their alignment to that Unity as their
highest ideal. So you see, there are many steps and levels between
the two and even beyond the higher one. But what you need to
convey in this sharing is that the human is the creative genius for
the planet. The human is the source of such wondrous beauty and
such despicable disharmony.

And it is all of choice: choice in ignorance of, or responsibility to
one's innate power, choice in ignorance of the Earth where there
is discord and lack of harmony, choice in taking the ultimate
responsibility for life and its expression as God's eyes looking
out through your own. Imagine God saying "this job is too big
for me!" It wouldn't happen! And so the human who is God, is
responsible and aligned to the greater Truth. Abundance flows
from that alignment to Unity and the awareness of choice. So,

---

5   Some words from Jesus on victim consciousness: *So don't tip toe*
     around those in victim consciousness, even though their defensive
     wrath can be vehement. Be compassionate and direct and hold
     them accountable to their thoughts about what has happened,
     what might happen and who is to be held accountable at the very
     source of its creation. Ultimately the greatest gift one can give
     another is to usher them beyond the trap of victim consciousness.

perhaps this gives a taste of what is possible in the world to come! Namaste we are One and so it is.

This points to a very different way of living, where one sees life from God's perspective. We see with unconditionally loving eyes, we realize the potency of our thoughts and we are rooted in an all-powerful perspective. A higher octave creative opportunity is present when we are based in Unity Consciousness or wholeness, as opposed to separation from everything.

This higher potential can seem like it is something that we must acquire or add to ourselves like a hat. In Truth, the Mind of God is accessed by quieting our human mind and its ego based commentary. If we can quiet our mind, it is like we remove the barrier within us to God's Mind. We then live from Love, which is the same frequency of God and thus we allow God's expression to come through us.

God knows only perfection and so as we train ourselves to see through God's eyes, we accept life itself as a *perfect* process and thus we are creating a more perfect result. Everything that is 'out there' is a result of our own ideas about the world. So as we focus on perfection and live with the assumption that everything is perfect *already*, we have a sure formula for a quiet mind because right now we are constantly judging everything we see.

The world is malleable to our thoughts and ideas about it. Sure there are things out there we don't like, but as we focus upon what we *don't* like as something that is 'wrong' about the world, we empower it and thus create more of it. We separate ourselves further from thinking as God. Our forebodings and worries put us outside the potential of Godly perfection that is held within the energy of Love and acceptance of 'what is' presently right here now. If we focus on something that we don't like as the 'perfect result' of the forces that created it, we are empowered to create in the direction that leads all parties towards a more perfect result.

Some people have an aversion to the idea of *perfection* and it's not surprising because our planet Earth experience is one of duality, where the very nature of our environment and experience is one of contrasts. So from the level of our human egoic self, seeking perfection has been frustrating and disappointing! The perfection that is spoken of here is *Divine Perfection*, the creative and real perfection of God, One or All That Is, and so there is no contrast possible with this One Perfect Heavenly thing. The perfections we have sought for ourselves on Earth are simply stand-ins for that Unity that we feel separated from by our human mind and by our engagement with the physical world.

One stepping stone to understanding this Divine Perfection is to imagine an energetic framework that exists within physical things. Energy exists like a three dimensional blueprint within the physical form. The energy and the form define the same thing, just at different levels of demonstration. So the creative energy that interacts within the form is 'Perfect' and the physical form is the *result* of that underlying energetic design. So in order to influence physical form, you must influence the energy that creates its structure. We influence energy with our hearts by Loving, with our mind by thinking and with our bodies by our actions, all influenced by our consciousness or the perspective from which we view the world. So in thinking, acting, feeling and seeing only Unified Divine *Perfection* (or Love), we energetically influence the physical world towards such a reflection. Seeing Divine Perfection puts us in the Higher Mind, where our capacity to create Heaven on Earth is fulfilled. So our work is to rest in the Unified Perfection that is already here, present but hidden all around us. This then allows the 'Love that we are' which might also be described as 'Divinity,' to reveal itself through us.

Perfection Exercise: Take a moment and rest in the Unified Divine Perfection that is right here. Look around you with eyes that see only perfection. How do you feel? And how does your heart feel when you are living in the perspective of 'I am Love' and 'everything is already perfect.'

If we hold the point of view that everything is already perfect and if we accept what is right in front of us as the perfection of 'what is,' it becomes quite clear exactly what we need to do or not do; it is our *resistance* to life that causes our suffering. Jesus said it quite nicely this morning in our conversation...

There are no ways around the gift of this Life! You see it comes 'as it is.' It is prepared within you, from you, by you. Your life is a bit like going to a restaurant that serves one thing and had always done so, with your wishing for something else. You see there are futilities and there are wise choices. The wise choice is to choose Love, know it is all 'ok' and walk your way through Life connected to the Higher Power that is available within you.

You see many people think that the power source is in the physical items of desire, the satisfaction of hard work and in intense and unwavering focus. These items are not the source of power; they are the result of Love and allowing the true power to flow through you. So uplift your Life by uplifting your ideas about Life and the flow of things, people and gifts will be available to you.

Love and find alignment with what is presented in the moment and what is true now. When you love Life and all it has to offer, Life is the joyful experience that it was meant to be! Hold the 'Now' moment to you, hold your focus upon what matters most… your vibrational alignment with 'what is' and so there is no resistance in Life to the gifts Life offers!

For example there is the chance to be in Truth and focused upon the way things are or there is the chance to resist life's current expression and take no responsibility for it. So the chance now is to be focused upon and aligned to the true expression that is yours to make. Your choice to make the life grand is what allows its grandeur. Do not invest in the past or the future potential disasters of life, invest in the 'now' and all will be well.

Your choice to make the life grand is what allows its grandeur. Do not invest in the past or the future potential disasters of life, invest in the 'now' and all will be well.

In the present moment, we access all time and space and thus a higher wiser potential is available to come through us. I was walking the dog the other day worrying about something when it hit me that I should just be present in the Now and an inspired answer will come in its own timing. Inspired answers are the ones to move towards quickly and act upon.

3. EN-LIGHT-ENMENT

I would like to hear more about the enlightened human body that will inhabit the New Earth. Do you have anything you wish to say on this? Sai Maa says that we must bring the Light into the body, we divinize and transform the body, we don't leave it to go to the Light. How does one do this?

Dear One, the human vehicle is a vehicle for Light. It is a vehicle that has been damaged and dirtied by life, so that the Light cannot shine brightly through it. So your work as a missionary of Light is to shine up your vehicle, your body, so that it is a suitable vehicle for God. Make of your body a vessel for God. This is done by careful attention to your thoughts, your food, your energy expenditures and your Light quotient. Your Light is measured by the energy you hold. If you are vibrant and joyful, you are filled with Light, the continuum of Light flows down from there. And so the chance to be whole and pure and true to the God Self is your choice each day in your thoughts, actions and emotions. Remain peaceful in the face of difficulty and you remain clearer for the Light. The unity of yourself in the face of life's challenges will allow you to be a stable and reliable vehicle for God... well maintained, well fueled, clean in and out... it is really quite simple!

Step One: Parlor Of Unconditional Love
If enlightenment is a filling of Light, a literal and figurative filling of the human body with Divinity, Light and Grace, what is my role or my ability to shed those things that hold the Light from indwelling my body? And if I were to begin right now, newly focused upon en-light-ening myself, where would I start and what am I capable of making happen?

An excellent question and one that is present for many people who are facing life on Earth right now. What is the road that will lead to the richness of human embodiment as God? The revealing of this state of Self hood is one where the human must step down from the pedestal of 'it is only about and for me,' and be willing to engage life from the level that is equal with those around them. This is a big step for some and not so for others.

This is Step One: Reveal to yourself the part of yourself that has NO INTEREST in such equality, this is your work, to notice and acknowledge this separate self and be ok with it. Do not judge it, simply acknowledge that you have a self that is not interested in a life where the life of others is valued like your own. After this aspect of yourself is noticed and acknowledged, then there is a process of welcoming this self into your inner sanctum... "Come into my abode, come into my parlor, come in and rest in this place of safety and love. There is no one here to harm you, no one who will criticize you, just come in." As you invite this to be your abode or a safe haven, something will reveal itself to your mind that was hidden before. We will not say more, we simply invite you to partake in this exercise of noticing yourself. Notice that you are resisting and 'be with' that part of self that is in this state. We say to you, that is enough for now. Namaste we are One.

Well who would guess that I would have the opportunity to practice this so soon! I went to a movie on a good friend's recommendation. I normally ask if there is violence in the movie but this time I didn't. I went to the movie later on in the same day I spoke of Step One (above) with Jesus. I have never been to a violent movie before because fearful images stay in my mind. I prefer not to let a Hollywood production taint my sense of safety in life because I project out into my world the potential for bad things that I have seen on the screen. For example if I am home alone and I hear a noise, I am more likely to move into fear as I bring up violent movie scenarios in my mind, than if I did not have the images in my memory.

So getting back to the movie, it was about reincarnation and depicted several souls interacting in varied life times in mostly violent ways. I covered my eyes and ears in the violent scenes and waited for the music to change, indicating that the violent part was over. About three quarters of the way through, I went to the bathroom, needing a break from the tension I felt and started saying out loud "fill me with Light, fill me with Light." It helped me come back to my Self and so I returned to the movie. Finally it ended, and I got in the car and continued to chant... 'fill me with light, then fill me with love, then harmony, trust, joy.' I sang freely, both in prayer and in creation of these states of being. The singing released tension from the movie violence and healed me. About half way home I realized that all the movie's violent images were only reflections of me. I was resisting them and so I needed to invite them into my parlor, the parlor of Love that Jesus had described earlier in the day to me.

What an awakening! I invited the scary faces and mean characters depicted in the movie into the parlor filled with Love, non-judgment and acceptance, where all are welcome. The parlor was warmly lit and filled with Love and Light, and from within that nurturing space, there was a unified perspective that took over and the roles of the dual world seemed to fall away. As mean and bloody movie faces that I had previously shrunk from entered into the chamber, I became more and more peaceful, I saw through them and my fear dropped away. The realization that anything outside of me could hurt me melted. My resistance to the movie dissolved and became gratitude. It was a revelation because I had resisted such things *my entire life and now I didn't have to anymore.* I freed myself by inviting all the things that I resist into my Parlor of Love, which I realize could be called my Sacred Heart, incorporating them into the Whole Me. I became so calm. I continued to sing softly and gently until Silence was present. I felt bigger, whole and Peace filled me like I had never felt before.

The conversation I had with Jesus the morning after invited me to continue the process: *So much has moved in you, it is a most blessed thing. For now we would enjoy for you to be still in yourself, to embrace Life as a whole event, where the despicable, the sordid, the angry, the graven are all part of the wholeness of things and are invited into your Parlor of Love. There is no real work other than this in a lifetime. The stillness that this brings may be cultivated as you re-pattern your brain and mind images to allow those things that are of that ilk, to be brought to the forefront and assimilated into the Oneness of Life.*

It is a bit like having some characters that are truly 'you,' left out in the cold for years and years. And this process is about inviting them in for cocoa and cookies and saying to them "welcome you are loved." (This will of course disband much of the animosity they carry.) And so there is no other work than this in a human life really for human life has been one of working against these forces for ages and ages in the work of survival and thriving on the planet.

So we say to you, Bravo! Hold yourself as One, at ease in Love and joy and this will be the completion of a life of fear and anger. As you invite all those who would be your enemy, both self-inflicted, created and those 'others' to whom you are tied in resistance, there will come a dissolving of these forms that will make Life so much more filled with ease. It is a most joyous blessing. Namaste we are One.

Embrace Life as a whole event, where the despicable, the sordid, the angry, the graven are all part of the wholeness of things and are invited into your Parlor of Love. There is no real work other than this in a lifetime.

I got back in bed and curled up to follow through with this invitation to freedom! I invited into my Parlor of Love the things I resist and shrink from… genetically modified food, head lice, all murderers, thieves and rapists that I have imagined in the shadows, politicians and corporations that scare me, violent video games, the villain from a movie I walked out of with my mother when I was 8 (the villain immediately took off his scary mask upon entering), etc... I am still enjoying adding to the list as things come to my awareness. It is actually kind of like a treasure hunt!

Parlor of Love Exercise: Invite into your Parlor of Love all things you resist, fear, hate and are attached to and in welcoming them without judgment, you are FREE! Some repetitions of this exercise may be needed.

Step Two: See Yourself Everywhere You Go

Jesus continued: *Step two might look like this... arriving at your own door, you let yourself in and are greeted by yourself. You move into the kitchen and see that you are already cooking dinner and part of you or several young 'yous' are eating dinner at the table already. The step after welcoming yourselves into the Parlor of Love is to see yourself everywhere you go. In everyone you meet, know them as yourself. At first this may be the personality self, but eventually you will grow to realize that the 'self that you are' and 'they are' is the great Self, the One. This expands your vision of who you are. With this practice, there is a rest on the journey because you experience beauty beyond words. It is like revealing something that was hidden, that is so familiar and so loved that it leaves you speechless and so you stop. That is what it is like to see yourself in others you meet.*

I need this reminder; I am still triggered at times by old patterns of impatience or reactivity. These strong patterns are perfect ones to bring into my Parlor of Love.

Step Three: Activity Within Calm

Is there a step three to en-light-enment?

Yes Dear One, come with me as I bring you there. This is a world of complete activity within calm, a world where there is no separation either at the mental or the physical level with the field of connectivity that exists between everything. So in this infusion of the active Self into the still Oneness, this stillness and activity exist simultaneously. The world suddenly becomes logical and clear. All questions fall away. The Truth that you wonder about and search for is revealed. You are no longer questing endlessly for the answers because you are the answer and you feel it in your body and your mind and in in your Love for everything around you.

So this step three: activity within calm, reunites you with the natural world while setting free your creativity and joy to LIVE in the human body and on this blessed Planet Earth. It means that things are done by a different standard; they are done with the standard of the oneness of all things. 'Will it uplift or degrade? Will it hold up under the Truth that all are affected by the actions of one?' So that is the way of the time to come.

How might one be available to that new way of knowing and experience?

In essence you are that already. There is nothing you must become other than available to it. By revealing your Self to yourself, you allow this process to unfold. Know that your intent to be active within calm is a huge part of this journey of unfolding and allows the very essence and core of 'who you are' more of your time and focus. Remaining focused upon your higher Self and the harmony of your actions with the unity of all, will assist your human self to be willing and help it to see the value in such a transition away from what was familiar in the past—energetically familiar.

You see, separation from God has an energy pattern, it is what the human knows and has experienced. The new way is different and thus will feel different than it has felt before. The 'being ok' with something different and 'going with it' will be something that will be appropriate as well. Like a new pathway revealing itself on a road that you have walked a million times, wouldn't you want to investigate where it takes you? This kind of 'open willingness' is what we speak of. The curious self, the child-like self, the willing self will lead you down this path to freedom.

Cultivate these parts of yourself that are active within calm and allow them to be strengthened. Use them on the path that you are on now by asking 'How do I feel in separation from all these people I am surrounded by?' And then ask 'How do I feel in union with all these people?' There is only a sense of coming Home when you step into this knowing of what it is to be One with all of Life. At first you may have to manipulate your mind to make this transition, that is fine, do it. Over time it will simply become more and more natural. That is all for now. Namaste we are One. And so it is.

Activity Within Calm Exercise: Practice activity within calm as you sit here right now and again throughout your day. Ask yourself *'how do I feel in separation from all these people I am surrounded by?'* And then ask *'how do I feel in union with all these people?'*

No Need To Feel A State Before Acting As Though We Do

Jesus, what is the importance of actually feeling or attaining a state of being like an emotion or a higher perspective, as opposed to just knowing it is possible but never having experienced it?

Dear One, the gift of Life in a body is the very thing you are pointing to. For you see, in the non-physical realm, you know of these states immediately, whereas from the physical body they are a mystery and new to the 'you in the body.' So the solution is to claim them and 'walk as if you were that' which makes the experience within the body a potential.

Don't you suppose that even great adepts who became marvels of spiritual authority, in their early days on the path were like you? Imagine they were frustrated and wishing for the knowing of the state that they knew as Truth from the spiritual side of themselves. It is very much a conundrum of physical reality that you must claim it to make it true. For you all have capacities that sit unused! Imagine having a whole garage full of tools and sitting in a pool of your own tears because you wanted to build a house! Wouldn't that be a humbling realization upon leaving your body that you had all those resources and you never bothered to investigate them or to try

It is very much a conundrum of physical reality that you must claim it to make it true. For you all have capacities that sit unused! Imagine having a whole garage full of tools and sitting in a pool of your own tears because you wanted to build a house!

*So the human's
preoccupation
with 'feeling' a
certain state is
a little pitiful in
some regards for it
asks for the result
prior to the action
to attain it.*

them out? You are a fully equipped garage of tools for building, healing, connecting, aligning and being. Sure you may need to read a manual or two so you don't harm yourself or another, but you are already complete! So the human's preoccupation with 'feeling' a certain state is a little pitiful in some regards for it asks for the result prior to the action to attain it. For you see there is no way to attain a state of being without having first witnessed its potential and aligning yourself to its inherent opportunity for you.

So with this kind of knowing, you may now venture forth as whole, complete and knowing there is nothing you need to add to yourself to be 'more' (in a spiritual sense.) You may take some skill training but it will not make you more—it will make you more skillful only. So realizing you are 'complete' is a critical knowing which gives you a sense of worthiness and uplifts your energy. So serve yourself by claiming those states of being prior to actually feeling them in the body or in the emotions and see what occurs for you in your life.

So if I want to feel like I am a fully Christed being, fully divine and filled with Light, I must then act from that assumption? I then live my Life *as though I believed it were true,* practicing Unconditional Love and healing in order for those capacities to be developed or revealed from their hiding place within me?

Yes Precisely. There is no other way! Doesn't it make sense that you would have to do it for yourself? Certainly there are teachers and others who can model the result, they have passed through this gateway and they are ever pointing at the door in a million and one ways. The human often has an idea of what the door is, which is erroneous! It is not the doorway of your dreams that opens like an Ali Baba gateway of Light; it is so much simpler than that! It is the doorway within yourself to yourself that you must find internally, in your quiet, in the stillness. In your willingness to stop searching outside of yourself, you will find it. Guaranteed! That is all really. We needn't say a word more. It is done. And so it is.

What is the role of someone who has assimilated this divine potential into their lives when they wish to help someone who is caught in suffering?

Dear One, The perspective of being God brings the realization of your God-hood. So as things come to your awareness... be as God. Be the Holy invocation of Love, be the higher authority in action, command the difficulty be removed, command that their eyes shall see. This is the God's opportunity and responsibility, to make it right for others who cannot do so for themselves. That is all.

4. THE GOLDEN AGE

Humanity is at a cross roads, a gateway of Light exists, where the land ahead is different. It is of a different quality and responsiveness. The human being who knows this and suitably cultivates their own Life and body to be appropriate for this New World, will find Life a joy. The human who ignores this and continues on bull-headed, unseeing, ingrained in old patterns and ways, will encounter suffering, for it is like a human who has learned the ways of the desert and discovers himself in the rain forest and refuses to change his way of living, it is a different reality. How is Earth different? It is filled with more Light: Light of the Great Central Sun, Light of the Divine Energy of God. Light is a marker of movement for transformation, for moving the physical closer to the Divine.[6] That is what it means that we

---

6   Raymon Grace, a dowser, said in his December 2012 newsletter that *"Energy is rising fast. Have been measuring it for 14 years and if my calculations are correct, it has risen about 1100%. That wasn't a typo, ELEVEN HUNDRED %. If we can accept the definition of energy as 'The amount of good that can be done,' then we have more energy to work with than ever before."* (Grace, Raymon, http://www.raymongraceprojects.com, December 2012 Newsletter.)

are entering a new era of Light: the Golden Age.

I wonder what the Planet will be like in the Golden Age of Light? Spiritual teachers speak of choosing Love over fear in our every thought and action. In choosing Love, we have the chance for rebirth and for Heaven on Earth to manifest. So it occurs to me to ask Jesus where are we taking off for?

Dear One, the gift of Planet Earth is a blessed one. She is a blue pearl, a wonder that enfolds the Sacred Life of the Christed beings called humans. It is from this refined perspective of Earth and the human family that the New Earth is given form or re-formed! It is seemingly attuned in a new direction, but yet there is more to it than simply refocusing upon Love over fear and competition. It is something subtly and yet boldly powerful. It is the realization of the human species as the creative form of God on the planet Earth. God is here as 'you,' as your very being and essences, God dwells on Planet Earth. As this becomes the known experience of the inhabitants of Earth, there is less judgment possible—there is only the allowing of Life to flow through the vessels of human form. It is not a difficult transition, but it is subtle because there are some tricky turns or needs for this change to occur with ease and grace.

One of the needs of this transformation is the need of Love to indwell the hearts of all humans. The heart must be awakened, vulnerable to the Life around and in itself. The heart holds the catalyzed potential of God. So with that glorious power and potential, it MUST be aligned in Love or there is simply a re-manifestation of life in competitive fear structures. This is sure destruction.

So what is it that might cause the human family to change so significantly? How might this glorious shift to a New Age on Earth be manifested? It comes as the many Light-filled humans that walk the Earth are brightened and shine forth upon those who don't have this awareness. As Light shines from an enlightened one, there is transference, an emanation that uplifts those around them. This is one aspect of the transformative shift.

Another aspect is the human living as the Christ and their willing surrender to this greater potential, primarily because it is what they are searching for and have been all along. It is what they THOUGHT that 'winning at competition' would bring them and never could. So it is victory! It is the human family in final reunion with each other and themselves, the Higher Self and the Self as seen in the forms of other humans. Transformation is possible as humanity sees each other with new eyes and open Hearts.

The heart holds the catalyzed potential of God. So with that glorious power and potential, it MUST be aligned in Love or there is simply a re-manifestation of life in competitive fear structures. This is sure destruction.

So much Grace and Love is flowing to planet Earth right now and for this reason there is no chance of failure, no reason for humanity to say 'we just couldn't do it'. Victory is yours and life will be new.

Thank you for asking that question, it feels so good to speak of it and to share the way to freedom for human life. Namaste we are ONE. And so it is.

Thank You. I feel so blessed in hearing these words.

From Slavery To Mastery

"Why do you settle for crusts of bread when you could have the whole loaf?"
—Jesus through my friend Hetty

Now is a time on planet Earth where there is 'change.' Upliftment of the entire species is in order and for that to occur, certain shifts in consciousness and action must occur. For many, this is brand new territory and for that reason it seems appropriate to share these new ways, standards and markers for a new society to be birthed.

You heard the story of Moses and his leading the Jews into the desert, newly freed from slavery in Egypt? Moses needed to remain in the desert for two generations, 40 years in order for the generation that had lived in the consciousness of the slave to be released and to allow the newer generations to transition to a consciousness of freedom, self-responsibility and choice. What is happening now on Earth is somewhat similar.

The beings that are now present on Earth are slaves as well. Slaves in the sense that they see the work of life as a burden; they are slaves to the physical realms and have been living this way for generation upon generation. It is a transition from slavery to the physical world (to masters of the physical world) that must occur now.

Humans have been living under the assumption that the outer physical world is the determining factor for the happenings of life, instead of the true origin within the heart, mind and body of the humans themselves. From slavery to form and substance, humanity has the opportunity to become master of form and substance,

It is a transition from slavery to the physical world (to masters of the physical world) that must occur now.

the actual means by which life has been unfolding all along! Humanity has been master of form and substance all along, yet the awareness and knowing of this Truth was not present in the consciousness of most humans throughout time. Those that did have this consciousness were persecuted in various ways throughout history. Like the seedling that finally breaks through the ground and into the light, a whole new environment is now available for the human family to step into.

The Great Awakening

This means that the human individual will find a new perspective as a creator God dwelling within the Consciousness of Unity. This is a step up for many and a great leap for some and will require books, classes, technology and other opportunities to shift human consciousness to a new level and amplitude of expression, where the human's very own identity is that of God, Self or All That Is, where the union of the human physical self is fully integrated with the higher energy bodies and divine expression. These aspects of the human being are present currently but not seen or integrated fully by each individual.

As humanity makes the transition to embody their greater Self in their own internal make up, then naturally new expressions of culture, society, family life, self-responsibility and education will follow. These will at first occur somewhat like a young girl who doesn't know she is pregnant and goes to the hospital with pains and is surprised to find she is giving birth to a baby! They will come on spontaneously in response to the authentic Heart centered action of people like you and me, by people at all levels of society with the Truth of Unity fully embedded in their Hearts and Minds, this new society is made real. Only as the human self is aligned to these massive changes in consciousness and perspective will true shifting occur. Humanity is already seeing on very wide scales the interconnectedness at the very practical physical, financial, governmental, and environmental levels. All critical environments, institutions and structures are fully integrated as unified entities and will stand or fall together. The interconnectedness is not something that anyone can say is not true anymore! So it is not a far realization to see that a change in attitude is needed and thus how one acts and the basis by which one makes decisions each day is changed.

So in sharing this work with you, it is best to offer the ways and means for these changes to be brought forth, both on a collective level and at the individual level of the human

The maps of the past will not serve the future at all. History was performed at a level of consciousness that the human family has outgrown.

family and in the home life. Now this is not to say we will not be challenged to return to old ways, we will time and again and the only thing to recall at these moments is that 'what I do to another I do to myself' and then it becomes quite simple what the best route to take is.

No Historic Maps To Follow

Not having a map to follow makes this time on Earth a greater challenge. The maps of the past will not serve the future at all. History was performed at a level of consciousness that the human family has outgrown. Competition in the sense of... 'my life is benefited or yours, but not both,' at the level of survival, will no longer be possible. The realization that there is only ONE of us here changes everything! There is abundance for all and it literally comes from within each of us. As we each open our Hearts to include the others around us and allow our true relationship as brothers and sisters to reveal itself by our actions, then something grandly inspiring is possible on Planet Earth and the New Age, the Golden Age is born!

Thank you for coming along for the ride Dear Reader! Thank you for your part in this vast unfolding story of humanity at the crossroads. Life is brand new and you, like a Lewis and Clark expedition, are venturing forth to find the way to explore the territory and to reveal the treasures of the New World. The very world that has always existed is now finally coming into its maturity after many years of growth and expansion. Like a plant that has grown large and bushy and each branch is thick with leaves, now is the time for it to flower, to burst forth in beauty, color and fragrance, as the opportunity for fruit is made possible! The Golden Age of flowering and fruiting comes by your efforts, by your willingness, by your Grace. Join me in setting forth to explore this new territory as we both create it and reveal it to Ourselves, our One Self! Namaste we are One. And so it is.

Envision The Future

In yoga class, the teacher Ann read a passage about visualizing the future. I have struggled with knowing what to visualize for the future Golden Age. If we are capable of so much more and yet hold a limited perspective, how can we imagine this New World? I lay there in Shavasana, the corpse yoga pose and St Petersburg, Florida came to my mind's eye with people hanging out along the waterfront on a sunny day. And in the vision I decide to walk on the water and I do. The people watch and say "how do you do that?" and somehow I convey to them how I am walking on the water. They try it and they do it too. Then some children see us walking on the water and as naturally as on land, they run out to join us. It becomes a sea of humanity of higher potential as more and more people see that it is possible and walk on the water. ... Now *that* is a world I would like to create and live in!

I shared this vision with my friend Tom while we were actually standing on the waterfront in the same spot in downtown St. Petersburg and he said "ok, go ahead, I'll hold your hat." That's the confidence and perspective that will bring this New World into being, that's the surety of knowing who and what we are. That is an embodied 'Yes to Life!'

May God's Eyes Be Thine Own

Jesus what must be in place 'within' one for this possibility to be real and for it to be shared globally?

Dear One, Know that this level of demonstration in the physical world is something that will come to pass, it need not be the primary goal for it is a symptom of what is possible from a higher referenced life. A higher referenced life means a life lived with the primary viewpoint of Spirit or Life itself. Life, the en-livening force, exists and is imbued within all humans and other life forms. For this level human perspective, acknowledge that it is beyond mere mechanicalness, a further ingredient for Life is required... this ingredient is Love.

Love exists in its fullest measure from the Godhead, the pure Source. And as one is seeing Life from the eyes of this Love Self and is moving towards the understanding that Life is something mysterious and available to us, then there is a greater chance for this higher reality to manifest. It looks like this... a human is God's formula of Self—full of Love in all moments of time, a Life-creating reality that chooses to be a demonstration of God's formula and potential.

There is no great mystery. There is however a wisdom that must come to and through the human so that the higher potential is possible. For now, your use of this information will set you in a framework of illusion and what might be better to utilize is the higher mental states and higher opportunities of looking through and living within the eyes of God. May God's eyes be thine own. That is the mantra.

Mantra Exercise: Repeat the phrase '*May God's eyes be mine own*' as you go about your day. One benefit of such a practice is that your thoughts, which are creative, will not be mis-creating when you do this.

*Just imagine
you ARE God,
what might that
mean? Practically
speaking it would
give you more
chance to create
than you have
used thus far and
you would have a
greater potential
to manipulate
material substance
and energy.*

I am interested in the miraculous or the state of *hypersynchronicity,* a word used in the book *Love Without End.*[7] I imagine it is life where there are *only* miracles and nothing out of Divine Perfection. Is hypersynchronicity a condition of being God and thus all material form and causality is of that origin, potential and opportunity? Could you say more about this state and if I have interpreted it correctly?

Yes, how the human sees determines what the human is able to see and experience. And so, this might mean a practice of using one's perceptive capacity or capability to see wholly as the God Self within sees. This is the Self that knows no other way of being than to be wise, sure, all-knowing and humble, in the sense of a child-like quality of Love, inquiry and discovery, although the word discovery can be misleading. It is not necessarily 'discovery,' it is more 're-discovery' of that which is already present within a certain band of energy and hence opportunity.

So in that knowing of Self as God and seeing as God, something more becomes available to the human. Just imagine you ARE

7   Green, Glenda. *Love Without End, Jesus Speaks,* Sedona, AZ, Spiritis,1999.

God, what might that mean? Practically speaking it would give you more chance to create than you have used thus far and you would have a greater potential to manipulate material substance and energy. So infusing the world with the energy of God through your thoughts and actions, another kind of world is revealed, more of a pre-dawn-of-time world in which there is benevolence, spiritual harmony, abundance of resources and the opportunity for Joy, fun and upliftment.

I transfer my identity to the identity of God, I reveal the God that I already am through this transference of identity in my own Mind

So your question was how to translate this into the world that exists now, how to hold this focus so completely that a state of hypersychronous action is available to the Life that flows through you. This is the grand experiment that is occurring on Earth. Can enough individuals move their center of focus and the bulk of their moments into this realm, so something greater becomes possible as a collective? This is why information such as this has GREAT value to the future of humanity, for it is the highest opportunity for humans to get some suggestions and focus for moving ahead in a better way than just bashing around in the world like a blind person, lost and afraid and hence insensitive to Life.

The union of the Self with the World is a part of this new state. The World becomes the Self and hence a playground of sorts for the grand experiment. I transfer my identity to the identity of God, I reveal the God that I already am through this transference

What if there were no victim consciousness, no illusion of separation, how would that make you and others feel? This is the potential of now, and as you claim this now as 'God's now' and 'your now' and 'Love's now,' something grand and wonderful occurs within both your experience and within the reality that you create.

of identity in my own Mind, a new reality reveals itself and makes the grand experiment the success that we all wish for.

It is not really an 'experiment,' there is a divine plan that was laid out with a trail of breadcrumbs for the world to follow, but they have been eaten! The breadcrumbs to this new reality were lost in the times past, when humanity learned to process information outside of the human's true identity of Self as God. This mis-understanding of self encourages false behaviors that simply create more and more suffering, discord and disharmony with all of life. And so, now is the chance for the true potential and purpose of human Life and the New Earth to reveal themselves more fully as willing vehicles for Light and Love! A World where the real Life of God becomes the norm, not just the possibility!

And yet as we say this, there is much that holds humans from this higher potential and purpose, both individually and collectively. That is why it is imperative for as many teachers and teachings as possible, to focus upon the harmony within the systems of Life as they already exist and focus upon the fullness of the human form as a God already. And so as you contemplate this higher or new potential, realize it is as old as you are and as new as this moment. It is fulfilled in this moment of your awareness upon it, it is revealed in a moment of clarity, purity and Love.

What if you looked out upon the world with innocent and all powerful eyes? What if your chosen perspective and cultivated reality was that of God? What if there were no victim consciousness, no illusion of separation, how would that make you and others feel? This is the potential of now, and as you claim this now as 'God's now' and 'your now' and 'Love's now,' something grand and wonderful occurs within both your experience and within the reality that you create. This means that

This is not a future possibility for some future self that is more schooled or more skilled or more healed or more loving. This is your possibility now.

something grand, wise and clear is available to YOU and we so wish for this to be your experience. For it is ours and it is what the human psyche has been searching for as it restlessly acquires and tosses the trophies of physical life on Earth. So Beloved Ones, this is your work, your chance and your opportunity RIGHT NOW. This is not a future possibility for some future self that is more schooled or more skilled or more healed or more loving. This is your possibility now. This is the way of Life that holds the human form as one Self, one wholon[8] of Life

---

8   Wholon, or holon, something that is simultaneously both a whole and a part.

43

as it exists on Earth. So be this! Know this Truth as God, Self and no other and something grand happens now.

So sit still and align your energy to the higher Self that exists within you. Surrender your ego's desire to know and have the answers and allow the Life to unfold. That is it, allow the Life to unfold as the God that you are. It is not to say don't do anything, it is to say do what you need to do from the perspective, authority, surety and Love of God. That is all!

We are being asked to eradicate the human self from the body?

Yes and No, humans need or think they need certain comforts, attachments and sustenances. This is true to the degree the human believes them to be so. If you could become a human that is forever embracing the God Self, then this transition is smooth. If you feel deprived, you prolong an opportunity that exists for all humans. The entire human family has this potential Now. And so there is only one thing to attend to: your own transformation and sharing this knowledge of the Higher potential that exists for each and every one of us. No matter what physical and mental contingencies you might have, YOU too are part of this Higher potential and thus may fulfill your Higher opportunity post haste!

The Golden Age: By The Golden Rule

So it sounds like this new Golden Age is one created from a different way of being, focusing on Love-based infinite possibility, not on limitation, but on Love! How does that work in the physical world, where there is so much that needs attention and maintenance?

Dear One, It is hard to imagine that moving through life in this way would result in a workable society where the needs of all can be met. If each and every person is attuned to the Truth that all people they meet are their brother or sister, then there is a different attitude present in the human field of interaction. The difficult part that you are tripping up on is the old thought that there isn't enough. What if the assumption was that 'All is I' and 'there is enough?' Wouldn't that take the pressure off situations that are unbearably challenging now? Yes there is discord, Yes there is a lack of willingness and there is also the assumption that the physical world is all that is. The truth is that spirit and humanity are creating what is seen in front of you. So pretend that there is only and always enough, that there is only 'One' here. Then what happens to all your urgency, all your determination to 'get enough?' It dissipates, disappears, gone. Poof! And so this perceptive reality, this process of seeing and acting from Unity is what is different. The standard, the gold standard is the awareness of Self as Other and Other as Self. That is as simple as it gets and as harmonious as it can be! So try that on and see what happens.

If each and every person is attuned to the Truth that all people they meet are their brother or sister, then there is a different attitude present in the human field of interaction.

'I Am All That Is' Exercise: Take an area of your life where you have felt lack and examine it through the lens of 'I am All That is' and 'there is enough.' Imagine that you are the other people involved and they are you. Try on the realization that there is only One here.

The Collective Rule

The Golden rule is *"Do unto others as you would have them do unto you."* In taking it one step farther to the collective, the rule might be called the Collective rule: Do unto 'the Field that connects us all', what you would want 'the Field that connects us all' to do unto you. Do unto Life, what you would have Life do unto you! What we feel, think and do creates and multiplies! See all others as you would have them see you… a whole, perfect, all powerful embodiment of Love.

5. WHO AM I REALLY?

It seems like this is a good time to bring up a couple of BIG questions that delve more deeply into who we really are and how this opportunity became possible.

I got an Email from my friend Les when he was stuck in bed recovering from surgery, (he always writes in caps.)

HELLO LOVE, I HAVE A COUPLE OF THINGS FOR YOU TO PLEASE ASK JESUS TO ANSWER FULLY, AS MUCH AS YOU WOULD ALLOW:

1. WHAT WAS HIS PURPOSE OF GOING TO THE CROSS IN SUCH A FASHION AND

2. WHAT WAS THE TOTALITY OF THE POWER RELEASED OR ESTABLISHED THROUGH THAT ACT...

AS FOR ME RIGHT NOW THIS IS THE FOOD I HUNGER FOR AND THE MEDICINE I NEED. TK U SO MUCH.

I suggested that he ask Jesus these questions since they were from him... He replied that Jesus had asked him to ask *me* to include them in the book, so I did. I realize that these questions put the entire process of human transformation into the Golden Age into a deeper perspective, and helps us to understand more clearly what Jesus actually did.

Our human potential is different because of Jesus and in understanding his life, we are more able to *become* that which he demonstrated... *'The Higher potential available to you now'*... illustrated beautifully by Jesus' life.

Yes Dear Ones, It is the time for hearing the Truth of this ordeal of a human body that is not the truth as it is told right now by the human family. The human family is misinformed in great ways around this event in history and it is now a time to set it straight. There is much to be healed and learned by changing your idea of what occurred and in seeing from a higher perspective the time that was spent on the cross as Jesus of Nazareth. What occurred in many ways was beyond the cognition of anyone present at the event. Even those of high spiritual attainment, if there were any, would find this event confusing. For there was no frame of reference within human life to put what occurred there into. It is the chance now to speak of it, for there is greater vocabulary and understanding of how 'Ascension' might be the potential of all lives, not the cross experience, the Ascension beyond the current human body to Life beyond the body.

Ascension
This is not a potential that most people would say is theirs, yet it is. The human is to attain the Ascension state ultimately, it

is simply a choice as to when it will occur. Many are being trained for this status now and many are not ready yet. It is ultimately the fusion, the full fusion, of the Spiritual Light of God, with the flesh of the human form, that creates an Ascension body, in ways that are not fully realized by the human of right now. There is a grand shift of consciousness that precedes this awareness of the greater potential for the human body and the full encompassment of the Light of God in human form.

It is ultimately the fusion, the full fusion of the Spiritual Light of God, with the flesh of the human form, that creates an Ascension body

The consciousness must come first prior to the engaged cellular transition to Light. And what this means for many is the training of the Mind and Heart and Soul to this end. Ascension is not the usual goal of a human life and that is why there is little known of this past event in its Truth, for it is not a reality that is present in the minds and hearts and ideas of life for the human family. And so this is the chance to introduce this Higher potential in the detail of elucidation that will here follow.

It seems to me that in order to convey this information in its fullness, there needs to be a framework of understanding about the human form and its native potential. The human form as it exists is partly matter, partly Light, partly energy and partly a prototype of God in human guise. (And as the human is cultivated, the human is strengthened and as the God is cultivated, the God is strengthened.) Jesus so strengthened his God Self, his identity as the God of Christ Conscious presence, that there was no real attendance of the man Jesus present any longer in the form at that time. This difficult gateway that the body participated in was one where the human form was transcended even while within it, even while present in the body, the body was overcome by the God Consciousness. It seems to me to say this most clearly: the human form is the shape of the being, yet the thing within it was different and it became different by the efforts and energies and practices and surrendered being of the young man that was called Jesus. That man no longer existed, what exists is the Christ presence through the form of Jesus.[9] That is the bottom line of this event; that the Jesus was no longer the one present. It became the God Self, the human form holding the divine essence and presence. The consciousness of the Christ Self was what was present in the body on the cross.

For this we mean to say Yes, all the human aspects of this experience were done to the body, it was done to the human body, but the human life had been gone for some time. The human had been superseded by the God Self and so the human experience was seen and felt through the eyes of God, a very different view or sight than through the eyes of man. This sight was cultivated and descended upon a willing form, the vessel of the man Jesus.

The Will Of God
And so Dear Ones, as you formulate your perspective on what all this means, realize that there was a process, a well thought out process that was required for this to occur. It will not occur

---

9   Note the present tense here, this very same One is 'speaking' here.

by the will of a human. It will occur only through the will of God. So as the God becomes present within your self, then the God Self may will such a thing. It is not a human will, it is God's will. That is quite clear. And so the human will is left wondering 'what to do,' how to assist, how to be a part of this grandeur and the only solution is the surrender of this self to the great SELF and that is all.

The true worth of such a gift is a Life newly lived, a Life that is of another magnitude, a higher order, a Life lived as the One Unified Wholeness. It is like one's body is surrendered to the greatness of the Whole. One's body becomes simply a part of all around it. One's body no longer is the fascinating topic and beginning and ending to the Life; the body is simply the vessel or perspective that God now views from. It may change in the next moment as the intimacy of the inner workings of another being are inhabited.[10] This shift of perspective happens with fluidity and ease and so there is a much different way of living and being than there is in the human form. The human is fully captive to the body, its defined edges, its activities, its needs and its demands. And so the New Human that has transcended this limitation is in a different 'room' in a different sort of experience, where the

And so the human will is left wondering 'what to do,' how to assist, how to be a part of this grandeur and the only solution is the surrender of this self to the great SELF and that is all.

---

10 As happened with Hope and Richard. (pg. 2)

intimacy with the inner viewpoint of all form and substance is available to it. It is like you become everyone and everything, depending on your focus and what you align to in any moment.

And so Dear Ones, be not daunted by this task, be ever ready to surrender to the Divine Grace of your Higher Being and know that as the body you inhabit evolves in its God Consciousness, this opportunity will come closer and closer.

And so God in Human form took the punishment of Man, there was transcendence in the finest and most perfect way. A new paradigm was made possible: that the God Self of a human was formed in a way that allowed a greater opportunity to pour forth for humanity.

And so the human that was put upon the cross wasn't really present at the crucifixion. It was God in human form placed there and thus the torture of such a situation was taken from the level of God, not man. And so God in Human form took the punishment of Man, there was transcendence in the finest and most perfect way. A new paradigm was made possible: that the God Self of a human was formed in a way that allowed a greater opportunity to pour forth for humanity.

The human genome was changed by this act and by the Divine Presence within the human form. It changed to such a degree, so that it is now easier for the humans that are here to do the same. It is like one person has done it... broke the 4 minute mile, broke the God /man barrier.

This Dear One is what your brother Jesus has done for you, made your Divinity that much closer to you and available to you, by his paving the way and his demonstration of what is possible from that place.

Ascension is what Jesus demonstrated. He says this is the path for humanity to take, each of us in the timing that we choose. It comes by strengthening the perspective of God within ourselves, that God becomes who we are. In the full surrender of our human self, the God Self takes over and Ascension may occur by the will of God, not by our will. By doing so himself, Jesus made this possibility real for us all. He opened the gate of the jail we were in, to reveal and demonstrate another opportunity that would not be available to us without his having shown us the way.

The Power Released
Les' second BIG question: WHAT WAS THE TOTALITY OF THE POWER RELEASED OR ESTABLISHED THROUGH THAT ACT?

Dear One, it is now the time to broach the next question, it is a potent one and for that reason it is well that we bring it to Light right now. The gift of human existence is something that is ethereal at many levels; the human Life is a fragile and delicate balance between the physical and the Spiritual Realms of Illumined Truth. And so the chance to partake of this feast of LIFE is required in a form of some sort, the human form is a unique and blessed structure from which to view the world as LIFE. And so Dear Ones, it makes sense does it not that there are certain structures of consciousness that are part of the parcel of the human life. The very existence of the human Life as a fortified and unified wholeness of creative consciousness requires that there are ways of being in the human that are different than with other animals and such.

The unique capacities of the human are very much the wherewithal through which the human is created human. Wholeness is a part of that make up. So what we are attempting to draw to your awareness, is the understanding of Life as it flows through the human body, and its unique capacity for the human, as part of the Unified Whole, to actually be the very Being that sourced it: to become one's own creator. To be the very thing that makes one what one is, is a very unique opportunity that exists within human form and function.

For the human to be born in such a way and to formulate the existence of LIFE within it, there is no capacity the human must take on to indulge itself as this, it is simply the law of nature and Life to make it so. What was changed in this relationship upon the birth and subsequent death on the cross of myself as the child and man Jesus, was a unique opportunity to transcend death while in physical form and function. To uphold a cosmic law and a reality of 'like formulates itself unto itself and holds the fruit of its work as sacred'… is the way it is gracing the page as words. The words for such a conceptual crystallization are precise and always inaccurate, for there is no representation in concept for this reality, that was made manifest so boldly by this being the Christ child. The child came forth in order to transcend a relationship that man had with Life and it so did. It came forth to formulate a new relationship with Life from within the human reality. It means in many ways and levels that life would not be the same on Earth now if it were not for him. The grace and flow of the life many beings lead now, beings that have taken advantage of this Grace that was bestowed upon the human family as the child was born, these people present now, would not be in this same availability to the Light they hold—without the Christ child's sojourn upon Earth and subsequent transcendence of the Light of human life to the Light beyond human Life.

It made no sense to explain it at the time to anyone, for they could not see themselves clearly from the distance of so close. Now, two thousand years later, we can see from a distance and it is that Wholeness that comes to Light. The Whole Reality is made manifest by and through and as the Human form. So it is that conundrum of being that which created you, being the creator God that brought you forth into form. It would be like in human terms, to literally become one's mother upon maturity to one's manifest destiny for Life. So the human gift of the birth of Jesus, as it was created and designed for the journey through man, is the union of the self with the Divine Self and thus the transcendence of the human life.

Hold this vessel of your Life as Sacred, as Whole, as the God space that it is in Truth and the manifestation of the Higher potential of your Life will flow through in the capacities of God.

The God Life was birthed through that event in a way that was not present to all mankind in the same way. And so we say to you, hold this vessel of your Life as Sacred, as Whole, as the God space that it is in Truth and the manifestation of the Higher potential of your Life will flow through in the capacities of God.

This is the Truth of the Human Life that God is thus ensconced and enthroned and there is no need to search elsewhere for this matrix of Light. It is within the human, available to all who search for it, cultivate it and demand it through their surrender to this Great opportunity. And so Dear Ones, this is the Human exploitation (demonstration) of the Life that was lead that must be exhibited by the human family, so that the gift and the manifested opportunity of the Christ child may be fully realized. For the Christ child came to show a delightful opportunity that was as yet unrealized to the human family and that is thus what has occurred.

Be The Christ

And so the chance to BE THE CHRIST is what the Life of the Christ being Jesus offered and demonstrated and poured forth into the consciousness of the human form. It was not there previously. The human until then was a servant unto itself and as the gift was wrought forth through the human flesh, the human became God in fullness, in reality, in demonstration! And so this is the choice for you who read this, to become this as well. To demonstrate your Godhead through the manifestation of this Truth in your flesh and blood life. To transcend the life that you lead as an individuated One in form, to become the Godhead in form, to become that which created you and the vessel of that which was created by You, demonstrates this miracle.

This is the answer to your friend's question and this is the answer to 'Why am I here?' 'Why was I born to this Life in human form?' When Jesus came and lived as he did, he changed the answer to the question of 'Who am I.' He changed the realm of possibility for the demonstration of Life as human form on Earth and for this he has died as he did. In demonstrating and returning as the Light that shown forth through human form and human imperfection, he demonstrated the greater reality of God in form and God in full perfection. And so this is the Truth, the opportunity and the wisdom that is asked of you who read this, to do the same. To make manifest in human reality and form, the potential that exists in this way, the next level demonstration of a Human's Life, that two thousand years ago was made possible.

To look at one's self right now and find the excuses of the inner drama to be the reasons for complacency and inertia, are fools words and fools wishes; to remain small and engulfed by the flesh of the human body when something so much more grand and potent awaits birth through you. This is what the devotees and gurus are in demonstration of in many traditions: the full manifestation of a greater potential for human life. Make it your Life, make it so. This is the choice, the gift, the reality of 'who it is possible for you to be right now' within your human form and structure—the God head that birthed you and created the laws of your Life, this is 'what is possible for you and for all.'

The Gift Of Life

This is what is asked of you now by your reading of this book. You are hereby put on notice that this is the plan that is enacted for your journey—your sojourn as a human form: to be the God that you are capable of so that it may come to Life as you have so freely done yourself. The gift of your life seems one that is taken for granted since you are here and alive when the True Gift is yet to be given, received or made manifest—you as the God that

The time of the awakened Human, the time for the demonstration of the Higher potential by the masses, is now here and you are of the vanguard for this showing off of the demonstrated Truth of Human in God form and God in Human form, All One,

birthed your potential, demonstrating this higher reality through the Life that you lead, through the Love that you are.

For it is all about Love… the Self is Love, the God is Love and to come together as a real, True and Unified Wholeness, is the gift of this and many lifetimes. So much has gone undone, unsaid and unrealized until now. The time of the awakened Human, the time for the demonstration of the Higher potential by the masses, is now here and you are of the vanguard for this showing off of the demonstrated Truth of Human in God form and God in Human form, All One, all the great reality of Life demonstrated, individuated and yet Universal at the same time. So be it! Namaste WE ARE ONE. And so it is.

There is a lot to take in here. I invite you to stop reading and receive it in stillness. To become the God that created us will demonstrate the miracle of Jesus' offering to us all. *"To become that which created you and the vessel of that which was created by you, demonstrates this miracle."* This illustrates the magnitude of the transformation that we have already been groomed for, it's like a house becoming the carpenter who built it or a sculpture becoming the artist who created it, or the child becoming its own mother that birthed it or a woman becoming the God that created all women (like Sai Maa!). A profound opportunity, something other worldly that was brought forth from a Higher potential onto this level, to uplift that which is here yet caught in its own web of misunderstanding. It seems a bit like Jesus' throwing a ladder down to humanity, trapped in a place they can't get out of... not an inaccurate description of our dear Planet Earth being given the Higher potential that is described here.

The answer to Question One was the assimilation of God's Light into the Human body, thus transcending death. Question Two was to become the God that created you, with the idea that you then have the opportunity to Give God Life, essentially you give your Life back to God. And then actively participate as God in the human body on the school room and playground of Earth. Sounds quite a bit like a return to Heaven on Earth—a modern Heaven of new magnitude, possibility and transformational potential.

A God's Life

I can imagine that living Life at the magnitude of God, but still having the lingering perspective of a human could feel like being on a bus careening out of control. This may be where the saying that 'Life begins on the edge of your comfort zone' comes from. Craig Hamilton speaks of the Evolutionary Impulse as it works through one's life; one is living from an edge that is not comfortable because we are moving into territory in the Self that is new.[11] Will you clarify this?

---

11 Craig Hamilton's Principles of Evolutionary culture, which includes: If We're Not Uncomfortable, We're Probably Not Evolving. Available on this web page: http://www.integralenlightenment. com/pages/articles/index.php?id=763899701

*As you embody
the God Self that
you are, the set of
Laws by which you
live, transcends
the laws you have
lived by.*

*Yes of course, the way of Life when
one is living as God, is a way that
is ordained by the laws of a greater
Life, a greater reality. The laws of
nature fall into this realm.[12] When
one lives from the human mind and
heart and body, one lives within the
human's laws of limitation... that
there is not enough for all and that
the human life is one of toil and hard
work. These are human ideas of life
and create a very human level reality
and life structure. As you embody the God Self that you are, the
set of Laws by which you live, transcends the laws you have
lived by. For example the idea of lack, inability or misfortune
are human ideas. The God Life is one where the Oneness of
all things is the Truth and thus what is needed and properly
called for by one aspect of the whole, is supplied by the other
aspects. This means the World one inhabits and defines oneself
as, is the wholeness of all things, as opposed to the small isolated
individual human body. Can you see how living as the God Self,
the One, the Wholeness, might challenge the sense of safety of the
human? This is what the quote of 'living on the edge' is about. It
is inherently a part of that transitional zone where the human
is transforming into the God Self: realizing, testing the waters,
aligning to a greater destiny. And so Dear One, once one is fully
ensconced in the True Self as the wholeness of Life and living as
God, then there is an ease and joy and miraculous aspect of Life*

---

12 *"Nature is the created wholeness in manifestation of a myriad of
harmonious synchronous occurrences, that woven together create
planet Earth."—Jesus*

that was described previously.

Not unlike a snake shedding its skin or an amphibian losing its tail to become a frog, there is an awkward stage or an uncomfortable stage within any great transformation, where the leap to the next level comes as a leap of faith at some moments and so to describe any part of a way of life as easy or joyful, may not be accurate. It may take some courage to move to this level of God Self in action. The reality is though, that once a human gets a taste of this level of Life, the God Self in action, the true mesmerizing, inspiring opportunity of living as the One, the All That Is, the True Blessing of Human Form, then there is 'no returning!' No return in the sense that the human has no interest in the (former) isolated life, it must move forward into the full embodiment or be lost. The human self, the small isolated self, is no longer the end of the line, the finality of existence. It is like this—you are walking along a road and a vista opens up and surprises you in ways you cannot imagine were possible, so you awaken within yourself a desire for this greater vista of life, that is what occurs. And so Dear One perhaps this has answered your call?

Not unlike a snake shedding its skin or an amphibian losing its tail to become a frog, there is an awkward stage or an uncomfortable stage within any great transformation, where the leap to the next level comes as a leap of faith at some moments and so to describe any part of a way of life as easy or joyful, may not be accurate.

Yes, thank you, that illustrates the landscape of God's world in contrast to a human world. When I catch myself in thoughts of limitation, I repeat to myself "I am not the body" because in truth, I am so much more, and from the perspective of the God Self, the body is simply one avenue for interacting in the world.

Release Of Birth And Death

My friend Les is having an experience, where he is in such pain that he has no choice but to hold his Self-identity as separate from the body. Jesus has said to him, *'the physical body is the body of death.'* Physical matter by its nature and identity as such is caught in the cycle of birth and death. Jesus, could you please speak about extricating oneself from the birth and death cycle and dis-identification with 'the body as my Self?'

Dear One, It would seem to be a simple process to extricate and disentangle the True Self from the body. This True Self is not so much attached to the body emotionally; the body is simply a vehicle for the passage on Earth. The human as it is entangled with the body, is stuck to the time line of Earth and thus is lost to the greater possibilities. The real question for you and others is to find out how to align yourself with your 'True Identity,' the identity that is not attached so much to the body. This is a challenge for there are few impetus strong enough, other than trauma, pain or true death to do this, although there are experiences of ecstasy where this is the result too. But for many people, the difficulties of life are the springboard to this kind of release.

This means that there is a chance for those who approach life on the path of healing to do this as well. It would seem to be a simple exchange of energy from the love of form and body to the love of Life; a transference of attachment to the True Source, not the illusionary reflected source. This means for many to quiet the mind and become so still that this kind of mental or etheric manipulation is possible. The other way is to see through the eyes that hold the human as Self, not as self! This is different than calling oneself by the body's name.

Earth Is Changing We Are Too

It is truly an opportunity that exists for humanity in ways not experienced before on Earth. This treasure of a moment in time and space is something that much has gone into creating. The human has developed and evolved in step with the Earth to this threshold of opportunity to transform. This means that there is no real alternative than to assist this movement forward, for resistance is simply an admittance of one's obsoleteness and that one is no longer an appropriate vehicle to be moving through this environment. This means that the life one leads must be targeted appropriately, no longer in the ways of the past, but in the ways that are evidencing now on the New Earth. This is not a chance for the human to say... not me, it is a chance for all to jump aboard for the ride of your Life!

It is not meant to challenge you overly, it is meant to be a gentle and convincing change of frequency, identity and Light. This means that the human physical world becomes secondary and humans become identified more fully with the Spiritual World. This is not to say the world disappears, it is to say it is secondary, not first cause! The physical is not that which is the creator. This is not news to anyone, yet there is a reason for the slow turning to the New opportunity that occurs now.

*All that we see is
God, all that we
are is God and all
that is happening
is God, there
is nothing that
is not God, but
even more so, the
human vessel is a
vehicle by which
the God Self is
enabled to ACT.*

Quiet The Mind

The human brain is a recording and feedback device and it is over active in humans now. The path to quieting the mind is a necessary gateway to this changeover in your life's experience. So with this we say… offer yourself fully to the 'SELF that you are in spirit' and realize the human physical body is secondary. The physical body is no less worthy to care for, yet one must care for it at the level of spiritual healing to ensure its full and vibrant health. The healing of the human body is affected by physical substances, the human body and its vibrancy is affected by its Spiritual Light and its Spiritual Origin more directly and increasingly more powerfully. So with this knowing, the handle by which the body is healed and transformed is fully revealed… it is the Spirit, the God Self, the perspective that sees from your eyes and knows itself to be that which is God in human form. That is all, no more, no less!

All that we see is God, all that we are is God and all that is happening is God, there is nothing that is not God, but even more so, the human vessel is a vehicle by which the God Self is enabled to ACT. Not tied to certain ways and behaviors in the way of devic consciousness, humans have free will as a God should! SO in revealing this SELF, this empowered and unified SELF to yourself, the new potentials and possibilities for Life are revealed and set free! So there you have it. Namaste we are One and so it is.

I lay in bed last night and thought what would God do? God would do differently than what I have done all my life. I imagine God lives without limitation and with vast *"potentials and possibilities"*... Jesus will you speak about this?

Yes My Dear, it would seem that the way to be God is to enact oneself as a God might. In fact this is a fallacy in many ways for the way to be God is to allow God to be you, you cannot reach to God, God is who you are and you simply must allow its resonance within your actions, thoughts, words, etc. And so Dear One, enumerating the many ways of God for yourself, imagining this or that as being the way of God, is not the answer to this quest, it is simply another ploy of the mind to infuse the life with the grandeur that the mind seeks. Allow Life to flow through you and you are a fluid substrate through which the energies of the Christ or the Divine Presence work through your beingness. It is not a difficult task; it is the easiest thing in truth! In surrender, in One, in joy, in wonderment, Life happens as God through you. That is all really! And so it is. Namaste we are one.

"... *It is the easiest thing... in surrender, joy, wonderment, Life happens as God through you*"... I could get used to Living a God's Life!

The way to be God is to allow God to be you, you cannot reach to God, God is who you are and you simply must allow its resonance within your actions, thoughts, words, etc.

6. MEDITATION

"... Quieting the mind is a necessary gateway to this change-over in your life's experience." So what you are saying is that as we become still and quiet in our human mind, we are then able to change our life experience. So the gateway that we are seeking is inside of ourselves. What are we looking for inside of ourselves?

Yes, this is true; there are vast opportunities that exist within your internal focus. There is no way to find yourself that is in the outer world because your true unlimited access to life is from the inner viewpoints. We seem to think that when we have a body that it is a physical handle to take on life from. It is true the body has its usefulness—primarily as a vessel of adventure into experiences that the human has in the body. This is not the ultimate reason for Life itself however. Life exists within, beyond and past the human life of experience. So in realizing that the life you lead in the human body is really just a side car, you will realize the vast opportunity that your internal life offers you. Your inner sanctum where you may view the world from, in all its dimensionality, is what will grace your days the most. We don't mean to say you

> *What you create in this inner realm is just as important, even more so, than what you create externally!*

must ignore the physical body, what we say is that you might consider using the physical body as the vehicle to assist your inner journey more often. Through meditation, shamanic journeying and other ways, you will discover the inner opportunities and landscape of the inner 'you.'

Now what will also benefit this process is the realization that there is no separation between you and others in the inner landscape of your being and thus you have opportunities and responsibilities in this realm that are important to be aware of. What you create in this inner realm is just as important, even more so, than what you create externally! It comes before the external creation, because you think of something and then create it physically. Thought, the action of the mind on the inner landscape, always comes first. This action of the mind is something that is grievous in its untrained state and razor sharp and focused in its trained state.

So the internal landscape's gate keeper, guard or bouncer of sorts is the mind. For the mind will be busy, busy, busy and not allow your true 'Life experiencing Self' to enter the inner landscape of your world if it is attracted to the outer world, to its manifestations and accomplishments for their own sake. (Which act like static on a phone line.) It is the letting go of the outer and attunement to the inner, that assists you to fully embody the potential of Light that you seek to offer the world. It is not quite a catch 22, but it is along those lines where you must let go of the outer in order to serve it fully! This means that you are the fullest blessing when you are not attached to what the outer world is presenting to you, because you know the 'Real World' is the inner world instead.

It is not to say there isn't a useful role that the outer world plays and that the outer world doesn't feel real, it is real in the sense that a hot flame will burn you. That realness gets your attention and helps you to maintain it as a priority while you are experiencing the body. What needs to be underlined here is the potential that the inner world offers in contrast. In the physical body what lies in front of you, in the place you inhabit, is your playground. It is limited. Yet, if you manipulate your awareness while remaining focused in the physical, you bring all of creation and time into the physical place you inhabit. So you and the physical have a greater capacity and opportunity for creation when you are multi-faceted in your awareness. Your inner landscape reveals vast opportunities and potentials to you! So knowing this, we offer the encouragement to pursue the stilling of your mind, which is the guard of your internal gateway! That is all for now. Namaste we are One. And so it is.

So it is almost like I must charm the guard or hypnotize it in order to sneak through the gateway. But actually I think it is enlisting the guard, refocusing the guard so that the mind is my ally, not my enemy.

Yes precisely, this is the way of things for the Nubian goat. Yes, truly the Nubian goat-self, (the stubborn self) requires such a focus in order to bring about its transformation into the true Self. You know that saying to "get your goat?" That is a true reflection of this action you inflict upon yourself! You keep yourself from your greatest desire by not allowing yourself to move inward in

You keep yourself from your greatest desire by not allowing yourself to move inward in your life. So carving out time each day to venture inward, is a critical piece to full embodiment of the True Self.

your life. So carving out time each day to venture inward, is a critical piece to full embodiment of the True Self. This will be the most rewarding aspect of the journey on Earth in many ways, for it enriches the physical journey beyond measure. You have had experiences that have shown you this, have you not?

Yes, this reminds me of the time I fell into a place that I called the void. I was with a group of people all meditating together at the end of the day. We had all worked at various tasks throughout the day with the intention of 'seeing ourselves' or revealing our inner 'no trespassing' signs. So gathering at the end of the day was a wonderful chance to draw all that energy together in shared intention of internal quiet. I don't recall the leader's instructions, I just remember that towards the end of our period of sitting, I fell backwards inside myself and found myself in a place where I was 'me' yet I had no body. I was free of the body. I was just 'there' as a point of consciousness, held in a way that was healing and a great relief. After some period of time, it was time for us to complete the meditation. I wanted to stay there in the void. I came back very reluctantly, like a child being called numerous times to return from recess. I wanted nothing to do with the body and the human life, it was so much simpler and more peaceful in the void, and the human situation seemed so unnecessary in contrast.

Charming The Gatekeeper

In meditation, it is not the extreme experiences that one seeks, it is the charming of the gatekeeper: the mind. It can be a pit fall on the spiritual journey to seek the fantastic experiences or to cling to them if they occur. Can you speak on this please? I would really love to experience the void again.

Yes this is a good point. You must realize that the point of meditation is to train the mind. Once that is done there is no need to further practice, other than to 'stay fit.' The mind is what will hold you from your greatest work and your mind will assist you in your great works. So like anything, it may be trained. This is like trying to pick up mercury; it is elusive and cannot be done by coming at it straight on. It must be done by holding the mind as it is and allowing it to do what it does and just watching it. It is like watching a naughty child doing its naughtiness. After a while the child will stop because there is no pleasure in it any more, that is the way of the mind. It will slow down its

The mind becomes the servant of the inner being, the Higher Self and the I Am Presence.

offerings to divert your attention, when you don't take on any of them. If you just sit and watch it, it will slow down and join you in sitting... simple really. The mind is easily diverted and enlisted in other games too and in the fullness of life, there is no participation in the mind's games and diversions. The mind becomes the servant of the inner being, the Higher Self and the I Am Presence. God will have its way ultimately! That is for the true warrior to discover and to reveal to themselves! Namaste we are One. And so it is.

I love you! Your answers surprise me over and over in their clarity and wisdom. You shine a bright light to illuminate the landscape of life, both the *inner* life and *outer* life. Thank You.

Meditation Exercise: Stop reading and sit without moving with your spine upright for 5 minutes if you can. Observe your thoughts, simply observe them without judgment or seeking to direct them. *'If you just sit and watch, it will slow down and join you in sitting.'* You may wish to make this a daily or twice daily practice.

7. ALL HEALING COMES FROM THE HEART

The topic that seems most relevant at this time is the one of healing. So much damage has occurred on so many levels to humans as they have passed through the meat grinder of Earth! Such a shame for it was never meant to be thus! Nonetheless, moving to focus upon the healing of the mind, life and heart, there is a chance for the re-formation of the life that is collectively engaged in on Earth. It looks like this: Humanity in union with itself as opposed to opposing themselves at each and every turn.

What do you mean by that, can you explain HOW to unify oneself?

Humanity's limitations are self-proclaimed and policed. The human is the one who is making sure the limitations and the wounds remain in place, for if freedom from them were to be felt, it would be perceived as destabilizing. So the strategy is… to release old wounds, patterns and difficulties at a suitable rate and each human will choose their own path. Some will not wish to let go of the limitations that are so comfortably keeping them safe in their perspectives, attitudes and sense of belonging to a certain class or strata of life. This is unfortunately what many of the lesser classes choose for themselves, primarily from ignorance of who they truly are. We see the wise ones have this understanding already upon them and they are willing to break molds more readily. It really depends on the individual.

As you move through the day, put your hand on your heart and say "how does my Heart feel right now?"

So the question is how, how to release oneself from the old patterns and behaviors and wounds that are often inaccessible to the conscious mind. It is like digging for a small treasure in a large field, it requires special tools to make it a manageable job! The tool is the Heart and the way is to infuse the journey with the Hearts' perspective. As you move through the day, put your hand on your heart and say "how does my Heart feel right now?"[13] How does my Heart feel about this thing? And you will soon discover the places and topics where your Heart is out of alignment with your present situation, practices and ideas of life. So this is a valuable exercise to begin right now

Ask Your Heart A Question Exercise: *Dear Reader, ask your Heart a question right now. You may end up getting an answer you do not find convenient, but if you are willing to act upon it,*

---

13 I only realize now that this is what Richard did with me at the Denver gathering (pg. 3). My above question to Jesus was "how do we unify ourself?" The result of Richard's questioning me, using that technique, created unity within me, which allowed me to 'be the Love that I am.' So I can say from first-hand experience that it works!

you will reap great fruits. So begin…

Is it really that simple? What about when the answer really counters your expectations and current practices?

Each situation will have its own truth and reality. The Heart is an arbiter of alignment with the Higher Source, the Self and thus it is a good place to turn in times of confusion or trouble. Remain connected to the Heart because this physical part of your Self is inextricably tied to your guidance, your Soul and your God. So given that framework for this practice, the true goal of your Life is promoted by connection with the Heart and so this is a part of yourself that can be trusted. We are not speaking of the human heart, we are speaking of the Sacred Heart, the very center of your Love, your Being and this is the place where these answers may come from as you use this exercise. Now with all things, perhaps there is a learning curve or perhaps you are tainting this information. Try it, see how it turns out, see how you feel as you work through things and examine the results. You needn't take this as gospel, you must try it and ensure its value to you. That is All.

So we have the check-in with the Heart practice, what else might you suggest, say for someone who is facing ill health?

This exercise of the Heart is one that will work in all realms of activity in human life, in making a decision… to take a job, move to another location, take in a partner for life and also in the little decisions of 'what shall I eat now,' 'what shall I do for exercise?' All levels of human question may be asked in this manner. One's Heart will not be able to tell you the directions of how to get somewhere perhaps, yet of two choices that your mind has laid out, the Heart will assist the selection of that which is in greatest harmony with the Heart's goals.

What are the Heart's goals? What is its role in our physiology and body complex?

The Heart is the center for healing. All healing comes from the Heart, that is why 'hope' is such a valuable commodity in human existence, for it gives the Heart the chance to continue on even as it is locked within a static vehicle or human psyche that may be entrenched in patterns of behavior that do not support it. So the Heart is the center for healing and as such it is a powerful force, for the Heart can call forth all manner of healing potential and modalities that other aspects of the body system are powerless to access.

So the Heart is the center for healing and as such it is a powerful force, for the Heart can call forth all manner of healing potential and modalities that other aspects of the body system are powerless to access.

Like what?

For example, the Heart is the aspect of the body system that is magnetically calling forth repeatedly those aspects of living that will heal the human body. It also calls forth for the healing of other beings that are sick, in need or otherwise compromised. The Heart is the part of the Self that reaches forth and pours forth its Love. Love is the healing elixir of life. It is a physical substance at both the human

*level and the Divine level and it is
the glue, the back ground music and
substrate of existence. So when there is
separation or sickness, Love, like glue,
literally glues it back together so that
the whole(hole) is repaired, the Heart
can do all this.*

*Love is what heals
and Love is what
renders the human
back to the Source.*

*You will recall when you asked how
you might help Lester when he was in pain and we said 'Love
him.' The way this works is that the Love is timeless, spaceless
and harmonious. It 'finds' its destination by your focus and
directly attacks any aspect of the physical destination that is out
of harmony or alignment with this State of Love. You see the Love
is the steady state, the true authentic wholeness of 'All That Is.'
So as aspects of the human create disturbances, the Love, like
a healing balm goes forth and reclaims that 'territory' back to
itself by healing. Love is what heals and Love is what renders the
human back to the Source.*

*Love is not something that is foreign to anyone; it is simply a
reminder of this motivation that holds all humans in its grip.
If you examine your actions, you are already a 'slave' to Love
in the finest sense! You are already motivating your actions to
attain, maintain, give, and receive Love. What these dialogs wish
to assist you to access, is another level or dimension of loving and
loving beyond the bounds of appearance!*

So loving is a practice that is healthy for me and others. It feels
like prayer, it needs no words, it simply is energy and a direction.
So I might be of service to my family, friends, co-workers and

others in my life by Loving. I could even Love the land I live on, the pets and the wildlife around me. I often Love Mother Gaia Earth each morning. Sometimes I watch the Canada Geese heading back and forth to the lake at sunrise and dusk over my house and I Love them too.

Love Exercise: I close my eyes and Love Jesus after receiving this and feel a wave of energy wash through me. If you feel so inclined, Love Jesus or *your* Spirit Guide, Guardian Angel, Buddha, Christ, Mohamed, Kahuna, Guru or God by feeling Love and intending that it go to 'them.' *'Love is what renders the human back to the Source.'*

The Sacred Heart

Jesus, the Sacred Heart is the Divine Heart that exists within us. It is an important focus in healing, in the Parlor of Love we were told to invite every part of ourselves that is not of Unity Consciousness into it. Could you elaborate on what the Sacred Heart is and how to locate it?

Yes, Dear One, of course. The Sacred Heart lies directly beneath the human heart in the sense of inter-dimensional space, it may shift in the human's perception depending on when, where and what it is being accessed for. In most cases, it is best to assume that it is in the center of the chest or slightly off center towards the human heart. It enfolds the human heart by its Grace and its physical vibration, when it is focused upon by the human self: it is strengthened as it is attended to. It is the portal by which the human might access the Higher aspects of Self, if the human feels like a gateway is required. No real gateway is required yet it can be a helpful visual and emotional tool to assist all manner of healing and focusing inward by a human.

You see, the way that humanity is programmed, in that there is 'only just enough' of focus and energy, and that healing takes a certain 'quantity of this finite energy,' when in truth the energy that is accessed from the Sacred Heart is infinite and highly flexible in its ability to right anything out of order or alignment with itself. You see it is a powerful laser beam of sorts that when cultivated might even be seen. So the human that can focus their thoughts and their energy upon accessing this powerful Shakti[14] and source of Love, will find that they are a radiant beam of Light and energy wherever they choose to focus themselves. The cultivation of the 'Sacred Gateway' is well worth the energy and focus it takes.

It seems as though the human might be lead astray by focusing solely upon the (human) heart and we wish to re-iterate: this is not the human heart, this is the Divine Heart. This is the Heart that aligns to Divine Wisdom and Love. This is the

You see, the way that humanity is programmed, in that there is 'only just enough' of focus and energy, and that healing takes a certain 'quantity of this finite energy,' when in truth the energy that is accessed from the Sacred Heart is infinite and highly flexible in its ability to right anything out of order or alignment with itself.

---

14 Shakti; divine feminine creative power or energy.

A connection to the Sacred Heart offers a chance to transcend limitation and to align to Higher purpose and coherence.

Heart that holds all power of Divine Healing and Grace and it is the means by which a human might find themselves attuned to the Higher aspects of themselves, even while in human incarnation.

You see the Heart is a gateway, a filter of sorts, that only allows Unified energy and information to be transmitted from or within this area. A connection to the Sacred Heart offers a chance to transcend limitation and to align to Higher purpose and coherence. So much more is possible in a Human Life when attuned to the Sacred Heart as a resource and 'energy vortex' in the Human body.

We say thank you for asking for this is a rich resource and so much is possible from a human who is attuned to this, it is like a portal to God. Namaste we are One, and so it is.

Enter The Sacred Heart Exercise: Thank you, there is much to work with. Are there any exercises or practical demonstrations you might offer to help us become *more* familiar with this part of our energy anatomy?

Yes, an excellent question, you encourage my practical application and this is good for the very literal minded that read these words! Let me see... Ok, how about if you find an area of your life where there is no harmony, where the humans involved are not in synchronous action at any level really. We invite you to then focus upon the Sacred Heart within you, enter it, become familiar with its feel, its taste, its scent, its color, fill it out in your sensory awareness to make it more real. Then, like the Parlor of Love, invite the players of your inharmonious scenario to be there with you, in non-judgment, in acceptance and Unconditional Love— not your 'idea' of Love, the real energy emanation of this 'place,' not something you must manufacture but what is present. If you cannot or have not felt the Unconditional Love, ask your Guides to shower you with Love, so strongly that you feel it and know what it is. (Stop reading and ask for this.)

Even if you don't feel it, it is done. Repetition of this request will bring this more and more strongly into your awareness. Much of this 'spiritual journey to wholeness' is not a sensory experience; it is a way of perception, a basis for action, a screening of your own Life through the eyes of God or Guides. It is a sensory experience on rare and beautiful occasions. Surrender to the knowingness that you are worthy and it is happening on many levels. You are the perfection of God's Divine plan in your form and structure, this is who you are already. So in focusing in certain ways, you direct the path of your life to strengthen certain areas of concern. This is one of the areas that will benefit you greatly to strengthen. It needn't be work, it ought to be a joyful discovery of something you already know and have just forgotten.

Much of this 'spiritual journey to wholeness' is not a sensory experience; it is a way of perception, a basis for action, a screening of your own Life through the eyes of God or Guides..

Unconditional Love Exercise: Ask to feel your true nature of unconditional Love and become still and available to the Love that you already are.

8. HOME AND FAMILY

Now let's talk about home in the Golden Age, what is it, how does it feel and who is there?

Dear One, home is like the saying says... where the Heart is. Where is your Heart? That is your home. It is not a place, it is not a structure, it is not necessarily a union of individuals, it is the place that the Heart resides, that is home. So much more is possible for the individual when the Heart is filled, loving and joyous! This means for many that there needs to be a slight adjustment so that there is an alignment between the concept of home and the energetic reality of it. If you live in a place that is not to your liking, what might you do to transform it? What is lacking within you and within it? Allow whatever it is that is lacking to be part of your present to yourself. In physical terms this might mean adding a candle to the table or a beautiful piece of fabric to welcome you home. Little things to uplift and feed the heart will help at the physical level. Energetically, there is the reality that so many do not realize, which is the grace that our family brings us, even as we struggle and resist. Allow the beings that reside with you to be those who you are grateful for. Allow their presence to bless you. Appreciate their offerings—as meager as they might seem at times. Appreciate and you will discover a wellspring of things to be appreciative for. It is a clever thing that reality plays a game with—in appreciating, one is filled with more reasons for gratitude.

The true food for the Heart is the love of God. The true feeding of a human Life is in service to God.

The standard one might use for determining if there is a need for transition to a different family relationship might be the question: How is my Heart feeling, even amidst gratitude for what is offered here? Is the Heart still filled with longing even in gratitude? Then there is an impulse to move towards that which will fulfill it. Not knowing what that is, one will have the tendency to look in all the places that it is not. The true food for the Heart is the love of God. The true feeding of a human Life is in service to God. As one can align the human faces with God, then there is true abundance and grace that can flow into the lifestream of those who work towards this manner of life. So Dear One, we see that the lifting upward of the Heart comes from the knowing of God's presence in those that surround one and then it is an opportunity to love fully, completely and harmoniously, even in difficult circumstances. This is thy grace and movement of a Life, fully formed and manifest. This is truly coming Home.

My Family Becomes The Human Family

Dear One, You wonder about the role of family. Family now, as in the near and distant future, is a springboard to many 'things.' Things in the way of harmonious and not so harmonious opportunities. Firstly, there is the richness of Life itself given through the human mother. Gifted by another human, the child is born to Life. There is no other way 'here' without it, at this stage anyway! And so the human self is born via the grace of the family. This is a gift never to be forgotten, for it is THE gift of 'LIFE.'

The second reflection of life in family is the opportunity to be a unit of a selflessness society, a unit that is a microcosm of the whole. An individuated presence of God's unlimited Love is present in a family, ask any mother and she knows firsthand the feeling of unconditional Love. This microcosm is a 'not to be overlooked' gift of family, for it is in referencing the mother-child relationship that more than half of the human population is already present to what Unconditional Love means. This is huge! And this is due to family. The work that exists in family units is excellent work for the world, for it prepares the individuals to understand compromise, authority and Love; all three important ingredients to a harmonious life.[15]

Oh I wish I had known this so clearly long ago!
Dear One, there is no need for regrets on how family has been for you. There are times in life where all the benefits of family cannot possibly outweigh the compromises one makes and thus the family no longer serves in the way it has previously. Like a suit of clothing, what a family offers can be outgrown. This is not to say the education that the family gifted is outgrown, it is simply the physical reality of it living together, being focused

---

15 Authority: the reference for one who is in the position to offer
wisdom and guidance within Love.

solely upon each other as 'family.' The chance to grow and evolve can be very great in family. So much richness, so much fortitude is created by family units. Think on the recent tragedies that have occurred, what about those families that served so beautifully to assist, uplift, harbor, shield and help? People seeking haven were reunited with parts of their families that they hadn't been together with much. This is the role of family, as well as to begin and end a life. That is one definition of family.

Family in the much greater sense is something that is of great value in the scheme of 'how to evolve into a Human Family.' For all humanity is the SAME thing that an individual family is, it has the SAME relationship in a spiritual sense, all brothers and sisters, all parents and children, All One unit, bound by Love. The evolution to the Human Family (of all humanity) right now is the opportunity to bring the tangible and palpable reality of this larger Family into the experience of humans all over the world. The choice to do this comes as systems are stressed, as storms displace people, as so much is challenged physically, the essence or spirit of things is revealed more fully. As the humans reveal their true larger Family to themselves, great movements occur that makes a whole world Family tangibly real.

So you are saying we are evolving to define family as all people. How is this different than say an old time village where everyone knew each other and looked out for each other?

It is not hugely different from a village. Yet in its idealized form it might have a more palpable sense of sharing on all levels, where no separation between another's needs and my own were felt. The unity is not out of a sense of duty or propriety in serving social order. The unity comes from the Sacred Heart's longing to know itself as Truth or One—through 'other.' That is all.

How might one know when it is time to move on from an individual's family? What are the signs or measures that might make it OK to break free from such structure?

Each human journey has its own rewards and challenges, so there is no 'across the board' answer. We will say that the human journey is one to wholeness. So as the humans themselves are made less than whole within themselves in a family, this is the arbiter or measure of value that may be put on continuing communication with one's human family. As parts of the individual are

And so we say to you, create family, create of the entire Earth your family.

required to be separated from themselves and are not allowed expression or inclusion in the family 'unit,' then this is what we mean. The journey to Wholeness, Unity consciousness (and other words that speak of this truth), is the Human journey. It is not one where the human self may be fractured and find its destination. Wholeness both within the individual self and within the family self is a supportive condition for health in this regard. And so we say to you, create family, create of the entire Earth your family. Treat the farthest one as you would your own child, and this will be the true Family of the future of planet Earth. Namaste we are one. and so it is.

There is a Hawaiian Kahuna concept of family that speaks to this great Family in an even deeper way. Kahu Abraham Kawai'I, said that "Family is everything in your existence. Everything you touch, everything you hear and speak, everything you walk to, come from or stand upon, every moment of your life."[16] It includes all aspects of the self... nice, not so nice, and they all are welcomed as necessary and part of the whole, the land you walk on, the tools you touch, every thought, word, interaction, they are all your family.

Family Exercise: Take a moment and think about how you define family now. How might you wish to modify or expand your definition of family?

---

16 Hrehorczak-Stephens, Tamara. *Abraham Kawai' I, A brief history of the man, the kahuna, and kahuna bodywork,* Tamara Hrehorczak-Stephens, 2012. (pg. 116)

9. WORK AND CAREER: TO RESIDE IN THE HOLY NOW

I often pick a card from one of my oracle decks. This morning I picked one and asked "what is this day about?" and it said CAREER TRANSITION. It's a card I get quite often, but it leaves me nonplussed, I am not sure what to do with it. Since I am writing this book, I thought that this was the new career. So I scooped the cards back into a pile and was about to put them away when I had the urge to pick another card, I hastily slid them into an arc on the table again. So I picked the card and it was CAREER TRANSITION again! "Ok, Ok" I said out loud, "I get it now! If I am to have a new career, what career is it?" And I tuned inward to hear "To reside in the Holy Now."[17]

So I am wondering how we can treat a child on the other side of the world as our own family, like you just suggested and still reside in the very present, time-averse 'Holy Now?'

---

17 'Holy Now': a phrase I later discovered in Glenda Green's book *Love Without End, Jesus Speaks*.

> *It matters what you do because your actions are attached to an inseparable Wholeness, that is the Unity of All Things at their Source*

What a wonderful question for it gives me the opportunity to share the profound unity of all things and all Life. As you reside in the Holy Now, in the isolated room or place that you are in right now, all life and all matter is affected. As you reside in the delicate formless and formed reality that encompasses both the physical world and the interconnected reality beyond your sight, there is an impact that occurs throughout all time and space. It is not something that the human mind can grasp easily, yet by attuning one's thoughts to God, it becomes possible. In attunement within the present moment of NOW, there is a way of being and interacting with Life that is formative and creates from conscious choice, by the Grace of this state of being itself. And so in attuning to the Holy Now, you ARE affecting, uplifting and harmonizing the entire Planet, and thus the Life and situation of a child on the other side of the Earth is subsequently uplifted. You are affecting all Life by your actions and your mode of being. This is the Truth and import of Human Life. It matters what you do because your actions are attached to an inseparable Wholeness, that is the Unity of All Things at their Source. And so in abiding in the present moment of Now, you are attuned more completely to your own part in that dance, that choreography of Life and thus are a force for greater order, not greater chaos on Planet Earth.

Well this seems as good a time as any to inquire about work in the New World.

Dear One, it is not a foreign idea, to 'be' not 'do,' it is however a subtle shift on how we have approached it in the past. What is asked of one residing in the Holy Now is to be aligned in fruitful cooperation to 'what is.' To be fully allowing the very 'yes-ness' of 'what is right now' to be here and to be attuned to your role in assisting it to a Higher Order.

So for example, say you find yourself in the kitchen, cleaning up, you do it without the wish that it were different, without your attention elsewhere, but fully in the present moment. It is Holy in that it infuses the earthly present moment with both the Divine Grace of what IS and what is possible. You see the Divine Grace and potential already exists in EVERYTHING, not

Absolutely everything is a Sacred Gateway to the Divine Order that it exists within.

simply in those things that are looking that way like: sacred objects, churches, altars and such. So, absolutely everything is a Sacred Gateway to the Divine Order that it exists within. So in picking up the lowliest scrap of trash, you might engage the Holy Now. In cleaning the dirtiest pot, you may engage the 'Holy Now,' a Higher Order of being and the field of energy that the human is connected inseparably to as well. So in infusing your every moment of Life with the 'Holy Now Divine Presence as yourself,' you gift the world, the universe and All That Is in ways you cannot possibly imagine from your human perspective.

So to be in a place on Earth where you can be in communion in this way, is a wonder and a healing opportunity. Imagine doing the dishes and healing the world! This is the true potential of

So we invite your awareness during whatever work that it is you do, to be in the 'Holy Now' while you are doing your 'outer work.' What you may discover is that your outer work is transformed by this depth and delicious engagement that you bring to it from this perspective.

a HOLY life. This is the way that the New World will be inhabited. Not a world full of doers alone, but a world full of 'be-ers,' being in the Holy Now! This potential is one that exists for all beings, for those who are practiced and able to hold this state, it is a blessing beyond imagining. So we invite your awareness during whatever work that it is you do, to be in the 'Holy Now' while you are doing your 'outer work.' What you may discover is that your outer work is transformed by this depth and delicious engagement that you bring to it from this perspective. So in truth there is no real answer to what work is to be done, it is simply the way that all work is done. This is the 'new work.'

Certainly there will be new lines of opportunity, new skills and technologies to participate in, there is no need to assume the world will be without these static aspects of culture and society. Yet they will be transformed by people doing them in the 'Holy Now.' So does that answer your question?

Yes I think so, although being so geared towards 'doing' requires a shift in focus, because old patterns, hurriedness and focusing only on 'completion' rise up.

Yes this is true, this path beyond is a path that must be chosen time after time, moment after moment. It is an illusion to think that one day all of a sudden everything will be different and it will be easy for one to make this choice. It is a choice-less choice for one who has embarked upon the path of Spirit, the path of being within doing, it is the path that brings the Joy that was so elusive on the path of life leading to here.

Are there practices that might help one to remain in the moment?

Always there are ways of doing things in a human body, it is the nature of a physical form. Physicality has it's orders or it's directions that assist it to end up in a certain way or place, unlike a non-physical reality, this is the case! And of course your next question is what are they? Well here is one... there are many that have been used over time, but this one is tried and true.

Inertia Exercise*: Allow yourself to be completely taken over by inertia. Allow nothing to pull you into action of any kind. Infuse your every breath with everything you have. Every question you have ever had, every thought you have ever thought, every word you have ever spoken. Let them all be in you as you remain stationery, alone, untouched by movement and action. This could be a meditation, yet it is a way of being, where there is no voluntary movement. It is as though you don't even have a body, and yet all of your life exists (past and future) already. This is a paradoxical condition; this will assist you to remain in the present moment. For it is so filled, that there is great depth and detail in NOW. Namaste we are One.*

Dear Ones, you may wonder what is next, where to go from here.

Enjoy Life! Enjoy the passage of time, the whiff of the breeze, the harmony of sight as it rests upon the mountain. So much is possible from the very moment in which you reside.

We say... enjoy Life! Enjoy the passage of time, the whiff of the breeze, the harmony of sight as it rests upon the mountain. So much is possible from the very moment in which you reside. So much is present in the Human Heart and Mind that is available to the rest of the entire galaxy. The way to access this richness in any moment is to rest in the Now, being who you are, a conduit to Divine Love and Light. That is all! Namaste we are One. And so it is.

Reside In The Holy Now

In any single moment, there is a full spectrum of how one lives in it, from the awareness of just the purely physical to the awareness of other dimensions. By taking responsibility for your thoughts, your desires, your intentions as well as what you hear, smell, touch or feel,[18] you have the greatest potential for serving Life.

The fullest expression of your human lifetime is possible by becoming aware. You fulfill your Higher potential by simultaneously operating at more than one level. If you cultivate a sensitivity to see beyond the physical world, to sense into the formless levels, in communion with your Higher Self, Life becomes quite a bit more interesting. In our awareness of the

---

18 Hrehorczak-Stephens, Tamara. *Abraham Kawai'I, A brief history of the man, the kahuna, and kahuna bodywork,* 2012. (pg. 41)

present moment and awareness of the world around us and within us, our conscious mind is in control. Until this awakening to 'now' is cultivated, we live our lives by the invisible programming of our subconscious minds.[19] *The way to access this richness in any moment is to rest in the Now, being who you are, a conduit to Divine Love and Light.* We now have a choice to live and 'be' at an entirely new level.

I Am Shiva

I am up at 5:30a.m. after returning yesterday from 'Shiva Nights,' a program with Sai Maa, where a large group of us chanted 'Shiva' and meditated all night for two nights in a row. I am woken up almost every morning very early to converse with Jesus on my computer. As I was getting out of bed, I found myself saying "I Am Shiva!" as we did at the Shiva Nights program. The power of those words carried me through the cold room, to the closet to find a warm jacket and then to my office, where Jesus began:

The gift of your time in the room with Sai Maa chanting 'Shiva' and sharing the energy of that space, that intention and the skillful means by which you were gathered in that way, is something that holds you in its embrace even now. There is no other way to say it than to say, 'YES' it is possible to be just that! To be the Shiva, the Shakti and All That Is. To walk as 'that,' to interact as 'that,' and the infusion of power and self-authority that this way brings into your life is something worth acting out. To know this as a potential is one thing, to know this as your True Life is another. This is the choice you make to stand as Shiva, always, only!

---

19 Lipton and Bhaerman, *Spontaneous Evolution*

This is the choice of a Human genome, this is the choice of Life itself! Life itself has the choice to be you at any moment and as you it chooses to be Shiva. For what other choice is there once one knows the lineup of possibilities? Live as Shiva or as the servant... the lowly human locked in flesh? No! There is no real choice in this, there is only the wonder of a Life lived empowered, not enslaved. Live as the empowered Shiva. Carry on! What is different now? How will you be? What will you do and say? This is the discovery of your 'now.' Your ever present moments of now will be Shiva's, God's, 'All That Is.' For Shiva is grand and powerful and smitten with all the opportunity of a Human Life and what to do with it. How to be in it, that is the question. That is the unfoldment of a Life—a Life lived in its fullest potential. And so what would Shiva do now? This is the question to ask.

And so what would Shiva do now? This is the question to ask

I stop typing and repeat to myself, "What Would Shiva Do Now?"... (hmmm, I sit and watch, and wait...) I look at Sai Maa's photograph and say to her "You have taken on Shiva." And I look at a photo of my youngest son with a bright smile on his face, being tossed in the air from a blanket by a group of friends and think "You, in your playfulness have taken on Shiva." And perhaps I need to see myself to see if I can say this of me and so I look into the darkened window in front of me. I see myself with tousled hair in the night's mirror "You are Shiva! What are you going to do with it?"

Tired from staying up for two nights in a row I say "Shiva is going to rest." I lay down and dozed for several hours. At one point I was aware of feeling like I was in a man's body, then drifted back to sleep. Upon waking I recalled the feeling of masculinity and was amused and astonished to think that the embodiment of Shiva would also have a physical component.[20] Strange, I do feel more manly actually, taller, less vulnerable. I asked Lynn my massage therapist if she saw a difference in my body as I lay on the massage table later that day and she said "yes definitely." I asked "how?" she said "it is lighter, it's like I have to hold it down on the table or it will float away." So evidently there was an energetic physical component of taking on the embodiment of one's God Self, facilitated by our shared focus and the intensity of our group practice.

God's Eyes Exercise: Look at your world through God's / Shiva's / Christ's eyes. Does it raise your sites and empower you? Does it make you more compassionate? How are you different?

Ascended Master Dwahl Kuhl

If Shiva were to get up in the morning and say... 'what shall I do today,' he would perhaps not be satisfied with something little. Work at the level of the Whole or Shiva, is best initiated from the level of your Higher Self. My earlier conversations with an Ascended Master named Dwahl Kuhl demonstrate work that he suggested I do for the Earth of a grand scale that would perhaps suit Shiva...

Hope: Dear Master Dwahl Kuhl, I am grateful to communicate

---

20 Shiva is often honored in the Hindu tradition in the form of a Lingam, a male penis.

with one that Sai Maa speaks so highly of. I am open to communicate with you right now.

Dwahl Kuhl: "We are One, the lofty I and the little you, we are One, there is nothing that separates us other than your ideas about yourself and your ideas about me. We are One, always were and always will be. And so it is! Your excitement for this time must be awakened, for this is the time you have been cultivated for, groomed for and awakened for. There is no other place to be in the universe than Earth for this glorious transition to Light!"

"We thank you and we wish for you to find the time and the place for very serious work on the Earth herself, in healing and alignment of her energy systems. She is coming unbuckled a bit, which is one way to say it, her plates are loose, her meridians are slack in places and taught in others, where too much energy runs in some and too little in others. Your work from the physical could be quite potent and assist the Earth greatly. You see the Earth has a very clear need right now for healing and alignment with coherent energies. The way for you to do this work is to sit and look at the map of the world, to align each latitude and longitude degree by degree. Follow along with it using your finger to keep focused and allow the energies that move through you for healing, from Sai Maa and others, to do the work. You are the conduit for healing energy that comes through your form and thus the alignment and stacking of the frequencies may be done correctly and coherently. So you see, we are so grateful for this help and wish for you to do it for a period of time each day."

So I began working on a map and later on a globe in my meditation space, just as he had asked. I did feel energy flowing through me as I did the work, back and forth along the latitude and longitude lines. A few months later, I checked in with him again.

Dear Beloved Master Dwahl Kuhl, I have been doing the work on Earth meridians, yet I need to have a meeting to update, correct and make sure what I am doing is the right thing… Please advise and encourage!

Dwahl Kuhl: "Dear One, you make me laugh. I recall the needs of life on Earth, the discouragement of work that was day after day with no feedback on its efficacy. For this you are blessed with a boon, I will paint a picture of your work, please take this literally for this is the Truth.

"We are One in thought word and deed. For those who walk the Earth, it is a more balanced and safe place. For we are One in our living, our bodies and on the Earth we all tread upon. What is now true is that the Earth is more harmonious because of your work. Earth is a brighter place, a more hopeful place and more healed place. Now what you must realize is that the 'work' on the Earth is a microcosmic opportunity and can be realized for all locations, events and persons. What each of us does, we do to the Earth. What each of us acts upon, we do it to the Earth. Everything happening all around us all the time is being done 'to the Earth.' So in taking time to sit and focus solely upon the Earth in a way of loving, healing and aligning, the

What we do to ourselves or the thing we touch, we do to others and Mother Earth.

Earth is a better more healed, focused and aligned place. So you see All IS One! (ha ha!) And the end is all good to see. We are so blessed and wish you to feel this in every moment, in every opportunity for sitting, for being, for Loving, know that all is well in each happening. And that we are One. And what we do to ourselves or the thing we touch, we do to others and Mother Earth. Your beloved Master, Dwahl Kuhl!" (A smiley man.)

At a later date, he gave me a blessing to say silently when I am in public: *"I call on the high soul that unites we two, to enact the great transformation in this life from human life to God Life, so that the union of self and Divinity becomes a conscious reality."* In doing this, it also reminds me to look through my eyes of God and I am benefitted: in helping others we help ourselves.

Blessing Exercise: Bless another in this way…"I call on the high soul that unites we two, to enact the great transformation in this life from human life to God Life, so that the union of self and Divinity becomes a conscious reality."

For a long time I simply did the blessings that Master Dwahl Kuhl spoke of. After a while I wondered to myself if the blessings were helpful. Some synchronicities answered that question.

December 18, 2012, I am driving down the highway chanting "Om Namah Shivia"[21] and I remember that I haven't done any Dwahl Kuhl blessings yet today. And so I silently offer the blessing to a driver of a tan car with a black bumper sticker up high on its trunk. I say *"I call on the high soul that unites we two*

---

21 "Om Namah Shivia" means adoration to the Lord Shiva.

to enact the great transformation in this life from human life to God Life so that the union of self and Divinity becomes a conscious reality." I think nothing more of it and much later, I missed my exit, so I took the next one. At the light at the end of the ramp, who should be there but my blessed friend in the tan car with the bumper sticker, which I could now read and it said... 'Heck is for experiences that don't fit into gosh.' (Not your usual bumper sticker!) Heck! Now *that* was a synchronicity!

Another time I walked into a crowded highway rest area and silently blessed a man standing inside near the door. I went to the rest room, washed my hands next to a woman and silently blessed her. I didn't bless anyone else in the place and as I walked out the main door, the man I had blessed, held the door open for me and amazingly

The fullest expression of the One Life is when it can act in two bodies as though it were One body.

the woman I had blessed in the restroom was with him, they walked out together. So out of 100 or so people, I had blessed two arbitrary people that ended up being a couple! Another time I was in the grocery store and blessed a man who ended up in the check-out line right ahead of me. The clerk mistakenly put some of my items on his tab and in his bag, which has never happened to me before. Upon discovering this *the man offered to pay for them for me*! I wonder how Jesus might explain these synchronicities...

Dear One, in the Unity of all things, it should not be any surprise by now, that the fullest expression of the One Life is when it can act in two bodies as though it were One body. These examples of unknown strangers acting in ways that harmonize with you are this very phenomenon in action. Enjoy this expression of the One God in many Human forms enjoying Life, Healing, Uplifting and Harmonizing with Itself.

10. UNION WITH LIFE

Dear One, good morning and Namaste! Today we will speak about the topic of union with Life. Union with Life is critical to an engaged life. In union there is a chance to be whole and thus the outpourings of one's life are both whole and effective. The union with Life that I speak of, is where the helpful, unified, and whole Self is brought forth into the human life, so that there is great care for the result or the process of the Life. In care for the whole, wholeness results!

It is not always thus, when a person wishes only for personal fulfillment, there is no Wholeness and thus an opportunity is lost. And so the union with Life assumes a certain attitude of Love for the process that is critical. When a person is Whole, in Love with Life and unified with the process itself, something magical happens that couldn't happen otherwise. The union with the great Self, in aligned purpose to the work on the planet, which is Love, results in Joy. The Joy that abounds at the birth of a child, the Joy of an individual upon receiving an award, the Joy of living life fully in complete faith in the process, these are the kinds of

And so we say to you, this is a time to examine just what your engagement with Life is, have you uni-fied or uni-died? If you are unified in Love, you are engaged with the Life and its infinite possibilities.

results that manifest from union with Life. And so we say to you, this is a time to examine just what your engagement with Life is, have you uni-fied or uni-died? If you are unified in Love, you are engaged with the Life and its infinite possibilities.

And so here is a chance for evaluation of your Life: How have I not unified myself behind the very process and potential of my existence? Have I held back, played it safe, un bound myself from the great potential of my Life and put myself on the sidetrack of comfort and ease? There is no judgment in this. It is however an opportunity to notice and make another choice perchance! For this moment in time is pregnant with the possibility for a way of life that is beyond previous understanding. And this is what we wish to awaken in you, in order that the great destiny of Planet Earth and human kind may be met. We wish for the result to be that which the entire human race can feel proud of. What is occurring now is something other! And so, this is the time and place to choose your role and to play it appropriately as a unified Self in harmony with Life. This is the role each of you play and thus each human is fulfilled, uplifted and harmonized with all of Life. Not lived at the expense of others or the soil or a way of living that is harmful, but as a unified and responsible individual attuned to the Grace of the present moment and the potential of Life at hand. This is all!

Jesus your words are inspiring towards action and yet many teachers speak of surrender, not being the one 'doing.' And yet there is that necessary action of the human-self in engagement with life's work and every day choices. Is there something to say on this?

Dear One, it is not only your choice to allow the greater Self through, it is your manifest destiny to do so, and thus as you make that conscious choice, you fulfill your destiny and the dream of your original spark of Life that came forth for development and evolution. For you see, there is a way of being that has been with you from the very dawn of time and to assume that it is any different than what is in the center of your being is incorrect. The essence of what you came from is still within you, perhaps utilized in a way that is not active, but it is there nonetheless. And so we say thank you for your endeavors on behalf of Life. It is a joy to observe the change in humans as they heal and uplift the entire human race. And so it is. Namaste we are one...

Is there something else that you wish to share in this space and time?

Offering of Self to the Spirit within, is a process that requires constant vigilance to the focused energy like the accelerator on the car. If you are focused on the accelerator of a car, you are paying attention to the direction and speed of the car. In life if you are focused on being guided by Spirit, you are very much focused upon your way of being. You simply don't do anything and everything from your usual human impulse; you are giving greater attention to the internal directive force and energy. And so, be attentive to Life moving through you as Spirit, this is the

> *The opportunity*
> *for Life is to live*
> *it! Live it in bold*
> *letters, live it in*
> *compassionate*
> *ways, live it with*
> *humor and Love*
> *and Joy. Live*
> *it as you would*
> *imagine a God*
> *might live, with*
> *great lightness*
> *and humor at the*
> *situation of the*
> *physical world.*

need of the hour. As you attend to this, you will find a greater result occurs.

So how are everyday choices and projects at work different when guided by Spirit?

The opportunity for Life is to live it! Live it in bold letters, live it in compassionate ways, live it with humor and Love and Joy. Live it as you would imagine a God might live, with great lightness and humor at the situation of the physical world. Imagine a God, fresh from the non-physical realms and what it might be like to arrive in the human flesh, with its needs and its tendencies and desires. Make light of it, appreciate it, don't take it so seriously! Appreciate the wonders of the physical world, the human body, the land of Earth. In an attitude of appreciation, gratefulness and upliftment, there is the chance for the decisions of Life to be made in harmony with the Whole, in service to the One and in union with the Great Self that you are. That is all. Lean in to Love and know that you are God here on Earth in human form.

I Am God Exercise: With you hand over your Heart, say "I am God here on Earth in human form." How does it feel?

11. EDUCATION

Will you speak about children's schools, education, teaching and learning in the New World please?

Yes of course my dear, it is not a different way of education particularly; it is a different topic and form. The general use and function of school is to assist the blended offspring of a society to find the common terms and ground for their advancement as a society. It is beneficial to educate in this way and we encourage its continuation. The ways in which it might be tweaked and adjusted, are in the topics suited for sharing with the children and the focus upon cooperation over competition… process topics that are not necessarily foreign to the systems now, yet the topics in school now are very 'end product' or 'result focused.' The New World is a 'process world' in demonstration of Unity, so whatever topics might assist the 'Wholeness within individuality' are to be appreciated and to be structurally taught and encouraged. The union of Self and 'All as One' is the primary focus. You see the individual life is a life of turmoil and suffering: in the Life of the 'Self as God,' there is a much greater opportunity and presence of Light.

And so we invite a new way of learning to bless the children of Earth. A learning that encompasses the very nature of the definition 'who am I'... the One Life living itself through each of us as part of the great whole.

It is another way of learning that is required beyond the human identification with the individual self. The human as God is in communication with a greater realm of influence; there is more at the fingertips of one who has identified the Self as the 'God in human form.' And so we invite a new way of learning to bless the children of Earth. A learning that encompasses the very nature of the definition 'who am I'... the One Life living itself through each of us as part of the great whole. And so the learning for children is done easily, gently as a collective realization. Each level of education in the systems of the world is progressively assisting the child to union with the Higher Self. Individuation and identity are within the frame and structure of the Wholeness, so then reunion of the Self in God is manifested through surrender.

And so this is the way of education in the future world, where the assumption of 'One life many bodies' is common in the awareness of humanity, working together to achieve Unity, wholism, and awareness of Self as other. Through the science viewpoint,[22] these

---

22 Lynn McTaggart's book *The Field: The Quest for the Secret Force of the Universe,* is an excellent resource for understanding what science knows about the unity of all things

topics may be brought into the main stream. It is simply a focus upon the Truth that holds forth from Oneness. That is all.

What about the many children that are struggling with the educational system now? Some are medicated, while others are finding it hard to stay within the educational system as it now exists.

Dear One, those children who are struggling with the school system are bridge children. They are bridging the world to new systems and ways of teaching and learning. They are one reason that school systems now struggle to maintain order and to produce the 'product' of an educated child. The focus is wrongly put upon the end product of a child, that is perfected at certain 'end product performances' as the definition of success.

What the true education of a child includes is full inner and outer training. The child is assisted to the proper ways of inner work, including

> *If a child performs well and is fractured within due to complete disassociation with the parts of himself, what good is he to himself or to the society?*

the unification of the many aspects of Self, whilst wearing the wisdom of God. It is not the truest sense of things to just allow any child to do as they please, it is best to teach children ways of knowing their inner landscape, their outer potential and their ways of finding union with themselves on all levels, not just the performance level. If a child performs well and is fractured within due to complete disassociation with the parts of himself, what good is he to himself or to the society? So the whole child is to be addressed. This must be a partnership of parents, siblings and the whole community as participants in this fusion of the child into the social structure of the community.

Give the children Unity Consciousness, the knowledge and demonstration of Oneness and awareness of remote affects, so that children will be catalyzed to become the blessed, performing and functioning members of society that the New Earth requires.

It is evidenced that the system at present is ineffective and requires change. The change might include allowing a greater breadth of individuals to access the schools so that panels of individuals from the community might teach topics of interest. Inner wisdom, Self-knowledge and seeing the 'self in relationship with others' might engage students experientially in ways and manners that are beyond the very dry methods that are used at present.

And so Dear Ones, the education of children is of great import and will determine the future of a society. It has brought this society to its place now and will regress the society if it is not addressed in its fullest and most comprehensive manner. Not only unifying the children within themselves, but unifying them with each other, so that the children that graduate are of One family, that is the only way that a future peaceful society

will be manufactured on planet Earth. Unify or die. That is the
harsh but blessed Truth. Give the children Unity Consciousness,
the knowledge and demonstration of Oneness and awareness of
remote affects, so that children will be catalyzed to become the
blessed, performing and functioning members of society that the
New Earth requires.

Do you have any suggestions on how to transition to this kind
of education? Everything seems so broken, it is hard to know
where to begin to transform the system that isn't serving the
society or it's children very well.

A society must transform prior to the schools' transformation. It
is from a whole society, a society that exists in wholeness, that the
educational system may be revamped. It is a predicament for it
is a 'chicken and egg' sort of thing. The gift of progressive schools
now within the system, is in their producing children that are
of a 'One Family' nature into the world, so in the opportunity
to perform as One Family, the unified whole is birthed. The
decisions of each individual, family, community and nation, are
then the factors that will determine the speed and success of the
transformation.

So education in the Golden Age is about nurturing children
to be whole in themselves, as a part of the school community
and the greater world. They will be taught that they are not
separate from the other students and from the natural world.
Schools will live the Truth that Family includes the entire school
community. They will teach the skills of self-awareness, inner
work, cooperation and compassion, so that a graduating class will
not only feel like they are Family, but they will know themselves

as part of a greater whole. This happens through acceptance of differences, non-judgment and realizing the Perfection that is.

Jesus said *"one life many bodies,"* so education moves to realizing and demonstrating a huge paradigm shift, by moving beyond 'learning how to think for myself' to 'learning how to think as the One Life' or perhaps more accurately 'surrendering to allow the one Life to think through me.' In order to do this, schools will teach inner wisdom, self-knowledge, self in relationship to others and the power of the human creative mind, experientially and in partnership with the community. Children will be assisted to experience the authenticity of remote affects, synchronicities and the power to assist themselves and others by thought alone, and thus will realize the power of the Mind of God in both experience and in concept. Children will no doubt surprise us with their adaptability to this 'new way' and greater perspective!

School Safety

After this chapter was completed, the topic of violence and safety in schools became the focus in the United States in response to a shooting at an elementary school. Please speak on this...

Yes, this is a worthy topic and a troubling trend. The symptom of unrest that precipitates such actions is truly a collective symptom, not of individuals with guns, but of an entire populace. No one may point a finger at another that has ever wanted to do harm themselves. The bible story comes to mind, "cast ye not the first stone."[23] And so what to do with this situation? Focus upon the

---

23 "If any one of you is without sin, let him be the first to throw a stone at her" John 8:7, Scott, Steven K. *The Greatest Words Ever Spoken,* Colorado Springs, WaterBrook, 2008. (pg. 477)

true cause, which is the heart and mind and separated identity of each and every one of us. Listen to the Higher Authority within you, allow the expression of your Self as Love to emanate through your actions, your thoughts, your very being. This state of Wholeness and Love is in itself the medicine that the entire country needs right now, the healing balm for a collective Heart in disarray and discord with Self. So enjoin your communities to pray, meditate, gather together with the focus upon Unity, on Love, on forgiveness of others. This will help move the collective resonance to a higher octave and a greater harmony within the hearts of those who now suffer and are caught in the projection of self through the actions of 'other.' When one sees the true cause within themself and heals it from the inside, the outer world comes more into balance and resonance with that state of Being. It is like the world is cold and needs heat. So in becoming a heater and walking among the people, you are the solution, your heat is Love,

There are no victims, there are no perpetrators, there is only One. One Life, One Heart, One Mind, realize this as your own Life, Mind and Heart and you become free of the challenges that face a human existence, you become aligned to the Christ that you are and always have been and thus 'the world that you are' transforms itself through you.

your radiance Forgiveness of the violence within your self and the violence you feel in 'others.' There are no victims, there are no perpetrators, there is only One. One Life, One Heart, One Mind, realize this as your own Life, Mind and Heart and you become free of the challenges that face a human existence, you become aligned to the Christ that you are and always have been and thus 'the world that you are' transforms itself through you.

Video Games And The Natural World
Please speak about video games, violence, creativity and connection to the Earth. How important is a child's connection to nature in the Golden Age?

This is an interesting question and the answer depends. It depends on the condition of the consciousness of the child. If the child is of Christ consciousness, their nature will naturally gravitate to the natural world, as the natural world will be their 'home' at many levels. In contrast, if there is a child that is not of this level of consciousness, the movement of the violent thought forms of video games will not necessarily assist their gravitation toward that end. So, if there are children that progressively isolate themselves within the confines of 'a world, within a world, within a world,' and do not hold any reference to the natural systems in life, there can come a time when those worlds no longer support the organic body of a child in human consciousness and the child's chances for proper development will be curtailed.

It is often the chosen path of a generation to counter the values and expectations of the generation that bore it. And so there needs to be that discernment between the separation of healthy generational needs and the human trend towards insular activities that are isolating in some ways. The huge trends in such pastimes amongst certain bands of society, do not necessarily in and of themselves predict a downfall. They can eventually awaken the children because the consequences of such a life lost in a cyber space world can be a catalyzing force to awaken, as can any jarring or consciousness-interrupting event. And so it is a worthy question with no comprehensive answer. The human life is one where choice is rampant as the children evolve to a higher level of consciousness, there will be many outer expressions of this manifested reality. To label all expressions through the computer screen one way or another is not appropriate. Is that enough of an answer?

What role does a parent play in guiding a child who has become addicted to such things at the expense of their health, energy and social interactions?

This is an entirely different question and we will answer it directly. The child who has found their way into an environment of the computer generated world and video game reality, is a child who has wandered into the forest alone. There is a chance that the child will be lost or eaten by wolves. As a parent, this is a situation that demands strong action and appropriate response. Children are not discerning individuals; they have not the brain structure or chemistry to suitably determine what is in their best interest.

The computer world, unlike the natural world that trained youth in times past and that culled actions and ways that were not suitable for survival, is quite different than the computer world. Nature was a just and harmonious teacher, the understanding and knowledge of ancestral patterns of survival were ingrained into the child's inherent knowledge base by the privilege of human birth. The landscape now is as different as the landscape of the first fishes that ventured onto land. No doubt many were lost, as the discovery and mastery of a completely new environment was taken on. This is what is occurring now on Earth, with children using technology that is regulated by humans caught in the web of separation, greed and with no natural checks upon their actions. Anything goes in that inner world of the computer and a child is unprepared to venture there, without some preparation or guidance. Do not hesitate to take a child under your wing and guard them from such a situation, if you value your child's life, their heart and their love.

What do you mean by that last line… *heart, life and love?*

In immersion in the world of technology, tension is generated on many levels, physically, emotionally and spiritually. This is because heart, life and love may be lost to a more potent master—a master that would steal these from the children of today for its own purposes and ends.

That is quite unsettling. So, if we are being asked to guide our children out of the woods, how should we do it?

There is not one solution for each case, for some it will be limiting time and content on the screens that take them from life, for others it will be in going in with them, to attend to the landscape that they are investigating themselves, so they will no longer be alone. For others it might be a union of concerned parents, who will limit time spent in this way in a uniform way. The solution may come from the system and framework that it stems from. There are also solutions not necessarily of the same linear solution set, but from the higher operating authority within the situation. For example, unify the child with their own higher authority to transform the child's pastimes. Make life outside the computer as compelling as within it, which may require extreme measures, and for this there is Divine creativity and Grace that will assist this.

Another way is by offering of the Self as the divine mediator in these types of situations. Transform your own relationship with the computer and technology and you transform the child's relationship. If something is of interest and irritation to you, it is something that you may invite into your Parlor of Love to transform it. To alleviate the symptoms in your child's life, the symptoms within your own heart, mind and life must be neutralized. This means to live as though this is not a problem for them, but for you. Fix it from within yourself. This is a higher order potential for many. For others, a more direct approach will occur. The Einstein quote of 'a higher consciousness must solve a problem created at a lower level' is what is being addressed here and we are grateful for the chance to bring this level of detailed help to those readers who find this a topic of concern.

Transform your own relationship with the computer and technology and you transform the child's relationship.

Change Your Mind And Minds Change Around You

Please speak more about how we can fix a problem that is seemingly outside of ourselves, by transforming our attitude about the problem from within ourselves.

Dear One, this is the question of the hour, for this is the way to true freedom for the practitioner of Life. See all happenings, occurrences and ways of being as 'my own problem' and forgiving them at this Source of their origin is the method we promote. It means to highlight the human role that is simply a participant as the One MIND and all humans are part of that One Mind and so to change your own mind from within the framework and perspective of the One Mind, changes other minds around you. It is a mystery revealed! And so in order for some to solve their problems with the children they see, they will find the solution is within them if they are ready for this level of inner remediation! It is a true clean-up of the human perspective and a retreat into the greater perspective of the One Mind or God, unified, whole and inseparable from All That Is. From this ONE Mind, there is only the Truth of Love, Harmony and Joy and so for the human to retreat to this perspective is the true destiny of a Human Life and will bring great Joy. A Course In Miracles[24] highlights this level of response to life. Namaste we are One.

Change Your Mind Exercise: Jesus said that from the perspective of the ONE Mind, when we change our mind, we change the 'mind(s)' around us. Think of a situation in your life where you are stuck at some level and realize that changing how you think about it would be healthy. See that situation from the unconditionally loving eyes of God. What changes within you when you do this? What does it mean to change your mind from within the framework and perspective of the One Mind?

---

24 Schucman, Helen. *A Course In Miracles,* New York, Viking: The Foundation For Inner Peace. 1976.

12. COMMUNITY

Jesus, what about community and how we live together and relate as individuals in society? How will it be different in a world of Unity Consciousness?

Dear One, the fusion of life with Unity Consciousness is a transformative and organic process that creates in ways that are beyond one's present imagination. The New World will be created as individually as the individuals who now form it. The difference however will be the many new ways that partner with the care for others and the unity within the Hearts and Minds of the populace. What we mean by this, is that there will be the differences you would expect in the ways and choices for how to live, it will not be a uniform society like in some cautionary science fiction novels of the past decades. It will be a society of individual choices and ways, but what will evolve through the consciousness of Unity is the caring for the whole whilst living within the individual body.

Caring for the whole requires an expansion of the realm of concern. The concern for the neighbor's children: are they fed

> *From the populace that knows through science, personal experience and education, the impact that they have by their thoughts as well as their actions, a new level of understanding will create a world of Unity and partnership, beyond what this present world has yet seen.*

enough, can we give them our clothes for warmth? Things as simple as this and as complex as using the other planes of existence while in simple conversation. Individuals will be working at all levels, not just the physical to ensure the care and upliftment of all humanity.

As you know, getting all humans to agree on anything is a bit onerous or well-nigh impossible even! But what will become evident is that from the populace that knows through science, personal experience and education, the impact that they have by their thoughts as well as their actions, a new level of understanding will create a world of Unity and partnership, beyond what this present world has yet seen. And so, it is this Unity within individual expression that will carry the human family to its next level of demonstration and uplifting expression of LIFE.

Many of us are feeling called to live in communities. The way we live now, in houses and apartments, like isolated islands side by side, doesn't nurture us as we would like. Is there anything you might offer on this topic in the way of guidance or encouragement?

The focus of the current societal structure right now is on isolation, attainment and abhorment of those who are different in any way of life. It is not a structure that feeds the true nature of human beings. What will best feed the human who is evolving to live in new ways, is to examine the reason for the yearning to community and to ensure that the community that is created feeds that need. There is no magic way of transforming the systems of life other than to create them, experience them and give them a try.

The difficulties of unified living come from the assumptions that people have about who they (themselves) are and who other people are. People assume that the other people are actually separate—yet they are not. They assume that their own and other people's choices are theirs alone to make—yet they are not. And so as the people who choose community realize the interconnectedness of all life, their choices will be more balanced towards the care and unity of all who are partnered in community in this way. It is a very different way of living and will require some leaps of faith that there is greater good in this form of living than there are drawbacks.

Some of the individuals who have created societal structures different from the current norms, are individuals who have seen

From Unity Consciousness, a desire for the fulfillment of others is born. From unity Consciousness, there is a fullness of Heart that is not present otherwise, this can be trusted. This can be built upon.

121

and felt a need and created something to fulfill it. It is these individuals who care and who vision another way, that should be supported so that there is choice. As communities are formed and sustained, the results will be their own indication of success. From Unity Consciousness, a desire for the fulfillment of others is born. From Unity Consciousness, there is a fullness of Heart that is not present otherwise, this can be trusted. This can be built upon.

The concern of many is that their generosity will not be returned and they will be 'taken advantage of' in some way. This is the gift of Unity Consciousness that this is not a choice for those who reside at this level of consciousness. Certainly there is the desire for more and yet the desire for more is transformed from within the perspective of God—for God is MORE! God is the ultimate Source of all, and so how can there be lack through God's eyes and perspective?

It is worth noting that the world malleable to your thoughts is something that has an upside as well as a cautionary side. Your status as a creator is true regardless of the direction of your thoughts. So in alignment with others that are aware of this truth, you will find greater harmony and transformation. Allow Unity Consciousness and the upliftment of your open Heart to lead you to places and ways of being that are new in expression on Planet Earth. Do it for yourself and for the future generations that will have the blessing to grow up in such places and ways. That is all.

Are there ways that we might transform our present developments, apartments and neighborhoods, that will promote such a transformation?

Yes, many resources are out there that will assist this trans-formation. Not only from the physical level in terms of buildings to meet in, shared meals and such, but in gathering to commune, to create consciously, to affirm the individual grace of children upon maturity and such. There are so many different ways to interact and commune in the consciousness of Christ. It is a blessed opportunity that now exists on Earth.

So many resources and so much enthusiasm for Life's potential exists within the young. Appreciate the enthusiasm, the ideas and the offerings of people of all ages within a community so that there is not a striation of a certain sector of community, but rather a whole community representative of all ages and ways of being. The wholeness brings strength; diversity brings both opportunity and challenge. Do not be afraid to engage with others that are seemingly different from you, for they are another you, they are simply you in different clothing. This is a leap for a present human to realize and demonstrate—it is what the grandchildren will know to be true and will create from. They will be the true creators of the new communities as the old understanding of separation dwindles and dies, then the new awareness of Unity of all Life will spontaneously and naturally create communities that are unique and heart centered in their acceptance and participation with Life itself. Life itself in demonstration though many bodies. This is the joy and the challenge of the times ahead. Namaste we are One. And so it is.

Do not be afraid to engage with others that are seemingly different from you, for they are another you, they are simply you in different clothing.

Communities of the new Golden Age, like the other areas we have spoken of, will be an organic response to seeing All as One and creating from that knowing. Embrace diversity, it can create strength in the whole, especially within Unity Consciousness.

The understanding that we are mirrors for each other is one realization that many residents of existing communities have found helpful.[25] When I find myself judging someone else, I now have to ask myself if this is in fact true of me.[26] Mostly I am chagrined and ultimately relieved to realize that whatever behavior I am noticing in another, is my own, played out by 'myself as them.' The relief comes in realizing the solution is not in getting *them* to change, it is in changing myself, which is easier on one level and much harder on another, because in doing so I must dismantle my ego's fortress of 'being right!'

Community Exercise: How might you create a 'community' right where you are, not in the sole interest of your own needs, but also to ensure that all those who you know or that live around you, have their needs met too? Is there a step you might take to make this real?

---

25 Wolf, Stefan. *Ecovillages and Self-reliant Communities in Europe,* DVD, Ringing Cedars Press, Stateline, NV, 2010.
26 Byron Katie has been a leader in teaching this truth.

13. FOOD FROM THE SUN

Jesus would you please speak about food, farming and agriculture in the Golden Age?

It would seem that this area would be much the same as the others and that an internal shift of the human perspective will shift it organically. Unfortunately, there is more attention that is needed in this realm, for this realm is the root that penetrates both the body of the Mother Earth, and the Human body. These two deeply interconnected and interrelated bodies of different scale, are inextricably entwined and needing similar kinds of transformation. The human body we will begin with first. It is the vessel for the God force and Life on the planet, it is not meant to be anything OTHER than this. Simply put, the human body is God's body and the human inhabitants of the body, in free will, are here to participate in this new way of being: at One with their Higher Self within. In so aligning and in collusion with the Higher Self, new levels of energy and Light are available.

The real concern now is in getting food of the right quality and performance that heals and uplifts the current body, structurally and biologically. In the future, the human body will attain more of its energy from the God head: the Source and thus the food as it is put into the body will be of a different quality and source. The food will be food of Heaven, food of Light, food of the Great Sun that resides in this galaxy. You see, there is a Great Central Sun, this Great Central Sun provides the energy of Light for all the smaller and more distant galaxies that surround it. When the human is aligned to the Great Central Sun, and attuned to the Source of all, then there is a new opportunity that comes to the human's body in the way of energy. This 'energy' is not of the same thing as you call it here on Earth, it is of a different quality and type. It is this rare energy that you are now not familiar with, that the human body is transformed and transcends the current system of food-in and waste-out. And so there is a new way on Earth that comes as part of a new Humanity. It is not meant to completely change the food-in and waste-out, but it will certainly modify it and change the focus that humanity spends all their time upon now. Can you see how the need for food, to have the money to buy it or to plant it and grow it, all take a very lot of human time? Can you see how the life of a human is now ruled and limited by this structure of food? There is another way of receiving sustenance that will become more and more common in the Golden Age.

It is necessary of course for the systems that provide food currently to be transformed, and this will happen from the Heart and the head in tandem. Currently it is the head and the pocketbook that create the food. What must be realized here is that food is an integral part of a healthy or an unbalanced life. As the human family moves to a more balanced food source, that is energy direct from the Source, a greater purity then flows into the body and so there is less need for the many other sources of denser food. And so, with this as your guide, ask me a question.

What does one do to access the energetic food available from the Great Central Sun?

Excellent question, the Great Central Sun is a source that is both local and distant in the same way that all are connected and there is also distance that separates. So in knowing of this Source in the Great Central Sun, an individual connects through the field of energy that surrounds all things to that Source. That is step one. This is done through intention, inner focus, gratitude. Then the next step is to align the body systems with the capacity to take in and receive that energy in a way that not only allows it to come into the body system, but to also be utilized fully and so there is a completeness to the receiving and utilization. This will occur as the human finds a teacher of this practice that has attained this level of actualization themself.

*The many ways of being in communion with the Great Central Sun, include the use of holistic therapies that utilize the energies and infuse them into various parts of the body, as well as the human sustenance through food that is grown in collusion with this energy. In working with the plants and the devic energies to allow the plants to imbibe this other level and quality of life, then there is an accelerated or 'amped up' plant available to be consumed by a human in form. This is not dissimilar to Rudolph Steiner's work with **Biodynamics**. Where the energies of the sun and planets are infused into the land and plant systems, thus upgrading them and assisting a finer product to result.*

> *So in moving into the new Golden Age, food will perhaps be the most profoundly different area that we speak of.*

So in moving into the new Golden Age, food will perhaps be the most profoundly different area that we speak of. The internal transformation of the human consciousness and psyche will pale in comparison with what is possible from this realm and opportunity. And so I complete this section by saying there are no panaceas to getting there, it is a gentle gradual intentional and penetrating process that the human must undergo to allow the body to transform at this level. It will not be the choice of all to do it this way, there will be generations that get progressively lighter and more deeply penetrated by this way of nutrition.

Wow, that is inspiring! Is it like being a breatharian? In *Love Without End*[27] you speak of looking at the Sun when it is very low in the sky, when it is either rising or setting so that it is safe to look at. You say that at the center of the Sun there is an "infinity point which will resonate with the infinity point in your own soul and this will give you much nourishment and positive awareness, even to the point of biological nourishment." You go on to say it helps manufacture vitamins and utilize minerals.[28]

Yes precisely, there are people currently in human bodies who

---

27 Green, *Love Without End.* (pg. 49)
28 Grace, Raymon. *Raymon Grace Energizes Water II,* (DVD)
A student of Raymon's speaks of programing water to provide him all the vitamins, minerals and nutrients he needs to sustain his body, so he no longer needs to eat.

have cultivated this capacity. What better way to handle a food shortage than to get it from the sun? No cost, no shopping, no cooking, no 'hard work' associated with this kind of nourishment.

Sun Exercise: Feed yourself food from the sun at sunset and sunrise, when the sun is very low in the sky and it is easy to look at it directly. Connect to the Great Central Sun through our Sun, through inner focus, intention and gratitude.

What better way to handle a food shortage than to get it from the sun? No cost, no shopping, no cooking, no 'hard work' associated with this kind of nourishment.

You didn't use the word chi or prana, is the practice of bringing in energy from the Great Central Sun different than chi or prana or is there another quality of energy?

Dear One, Know that the ways of the Light Era are different, there is an experience now on Earth that mimics this Higher Potential and the words such as chi and prana are fair assessments of this new energy, but they need not limit it either. As you know of these things now in your works and practices for healing and energy work, they have a certain reference and notable power of changeability. The new energy we speak of as I said is new, it has no precursor presently on Earth that humans know of. It is presently unavailable in vast quantities, but as the vibration of the Earth herself is raised, there is a greater magnetism for this energy to enter the atmosphere and infuse the human life and family of Man.

What one does to another they do to themselves. So as we pour poisons upon the Earth, we poison ourselves.

Not limiting it is what we ask of you. It is like this, if you are given a hammer and you have used hammers before and you know what a hammer can do, you will not try to use a hammer to drill a hole or to lift a house. We ask of you to remain open to not labeling, so that as newer energies become available within a field of energy forming on an ascending Earth, there is a chance for the fullest potential of these energies to be realized by NOT labeling them with outdated labels. As new energies come into your awareness, new opportunities for their use will be revealed. Allow this process, this newness to be one of discovery and revelation of those things that you always dreamt were possible, but never knew quite how to make them real. This is the time that you have been awaiting. These energies will be the playground for ones such as you, who wish to know.

Mother Earth And Farming

And what about the body of Mother Earth, is there a similar process for her?

Not precisely, but there are many ways to improve upon the current systems. The contact point with the Earth herself are the Devic energies that are assigned the task of fulfilling the divine blueprints. They are quarantined now by the difficulties incurred by the human use of manufactured poisons and other such things that are poured upon the Earth's body.[29] What is required is a new

---

29 Herbicides, insecticides, toxic wastes, groundwater pollution, fertilizers…, etc.

level of awareness around these topics; what one does to another they do to themselves. So as we pour poisons upon the Earth, we poison ourselves. This is a simple equation that needn't be 'added up' to get to the imperative that the human family is not existing in a way that is suitable for a 'God in human form' right now.

And our encouragement to you right now is to move from contamination of the Earth to collusion with the Earth. Allow the Earth herself to show you how best to farm. Follow her guidance in terms of finding systems that mimic her ways and methods. Ways that are like natural systems will best support this transformation right now.[30] There are no easy ways to fulfill the feeding of the human population as it now exists. And so as more and more grow their own food, the tension on this system will ease and perhaps allow greater transformation to occur. As the human realizes and practices the golden rule to the Earth, magnificent clarity and Love will return both to the Earth and to the humans themselves, that practice living in this way. That is all.

Feeding Our Changing Bodies

I often feel like my body is hungry for something and I don't know what it is, is it a hunger for the nourishment of the Source?

Yes and no, there are times when the yearning a human organism feels is for this great returning, it is not however a time on Earth to dwell upon this non-probability. It is best to focus upon the Higher Intelligence that exists within you and allow it to feed and

---

30 Back To Eden DVD highlights nature's way of gardening without added water or fertilizer, as in a natural forest.
http://backtoedenfilm.com/how_to/index.html

nourish you. Nourishment may come in many ways at many levels, the biological nourishment included. And so be not discouraged, but realize this is the transition time where the body is shifting in ways not previously experienced. There may be times of discomfort and dissatisfaction with the nourishment that you are familiar with. Allow it and know that the human level of perfection and the Divine perfection are quite different. Divine perfection has room for discomfort, even though in the full embodied perfection of God, there is only alignment and wholeness.

This is an exciting section! Imagine 'eating' the sun, eating less and less solid food; imagine the human body transforming to sustain itself from the sun over a few generations. Perhaps in the nick of time, as foods are less nutritious having been grown on depleted soils. Jesus speaks of more people growing their own food for its higher quality and to take the burden off of huge farms that feed the population now. Moving to organic and biodynamic farming will also bring healing to the Kingdoms[31] that live parallel to us and that are in charge of putting energetic blueprints into physical form. From Unity Consciousness, wholeness will reveal itself to the Earth.

---

31 Stodola, Michael. Author of handout on devas, he does energy clearings in cooperation with the devic realm.
    http://www.ablecrystals.com/contact.html

14. GOVERNMENT, WEALTH AND CURRENCY

Dear One, the entire human story on Earth is closely tied to government. Government is a result of the consciousness of the people in most cases. As societies rise in their culture and their higher authority over themselves and as they are more refined in their habits and patterns, there is a tendency to elect a government body that is not always in harmony with the good of all residents. It would seem to be a tendency of higher forms of government to exacerbate systems of living that are not egalitarian.

And so the truth is each man must govern himself or herself, each individual is like a State of Being unto themselves and if they are not regulated and reformed in their practices within their own mind and body, how might an elected body of officials be so? And so the government is one thing that must come first from within each and every citizen and afterwards beyond that, from the Hearts and Minds of individuals who form governments.

As a society attains the Christ Consciousness level, there is no need for government in the regulatory sense, there is only need for a cooperative community of individuals willing and able to exercise

And so the truth is each man must govern himself or herself, each individual is like a State of Being unto themselves and if they are not regulated and reformed in their practices within their own mind and body, how might an elected body of officials be so?

taxes upon the populace, to repair and maintain roads and infrastructure that is of the community. And so the human concept of government comes from the lack of self-government within people, and as this shifts to a Higher order, the government will be smaller and more compact. It will hold the humans that are part of a society to their own regulation, except for the needed aspects of community living. This is not to say there is not aberrant behavior and that issues need to be addressed. It is to say when a populace matures in this way, the government has a very different role and purvue.

The Rich Get Richer

'The rich get richer and the poor get poorer.' Is this true Jesus and if so why? And how can a poor person become rich?

Dear One, this ancient saying that exists in many cultures speaks the truth that man creates for himself. The reality of human engagement with life is that those humans who are poor of spirit, poor of gratitude, expansion and Light shall remain so. And those humans who are rich in spirit, in Light, in acceptance of their role in the great continuum, they shall remain as blessed and whole reflections of the Law in action. The Law is God's Law. What you think upon ye shall become. Think on God, dwell on perfection, and radiate Love and the God presence within you may shine forth. As ye would wish: as you wish (think) the world provides.

Allow Your Heart To Be Your Banker

Dear One, the currencies of the world are simply markers for the energy and value that humans place on things, services and agreements. It is not of the world of God to determine such things, it is a created system of man, to

Do not be curtailed in doing good or sharing wealth by lack of currency, allow your heart to be your banker and your Life will be abundant and joyful. That is all.

save time and create exchange that is efficient. If there are aspects of the system that do not serve the whole: refine them. If there are ways and places to uplift through the use of currency, make them part of your practice. Do not be curtailed in doing good or sharing wealth by lack of currency, allow your heart to be your banker and your Life will be abundant and joyful. That is all.

Can you say any more on exchange systems in the Golden Age? Will localized currencies, barter or barter currencies be different?

Dear One, the currencies of the future are no different than the currencies of now. Whatever way you choose to create that exchange, is the way that will be available to you. Do not be afraid to create your own currencies, it is only a marker for energy and life. And so there is no restraint that need be put upon such things. Whatever uplifts and assists the human family in its wholeness will find its grace and support in the Golden Age and what will restrain and curtail the human family will not. It is as simple as that.

Your Heart As Your Banker Exercise: If your heart were your banker what would be different in how you earn, save, spend and share your money?

15. MY LIFE? GOD'S LIFE?

Who's life is it anyway, mine or God's and where does the motivation and energy come from when there are things to be done and the energy to do them isn't there.

In the human continuum of life, there are places of human action and inaction, where the human is both desirous and yet powerless to enact the change. This is due to various factors, including the need for the moment to be the way it is because of karma. In truth however, the union of the God Self with the human self, and the energy that then flows through the human, acts like water to sugar. It melts the demand of karma and so there is a transformation that is allowed due to this higher energy that is engaged. And so to infuse the issue at hand with Divine Grace and Light, it requires the human to focus in the direction of the Divine for assistance—and that is what is required in this case: the realization that 'you' aren't doing it and that you need help. And so that is the message of the moment, that the surrender of life to the Divine aspects of the Self, are where there is a mystery revealed and an energy infused—and this is like a key to handcuffs. The entire life surrendered in this way is the ultimate goal, for there is no other certainty in a human world than the Love of God... the Divine Grace and flow of energy to the human life from surrendered willingness to be the vessel of Light. And so we reveal these secrets to you so that there is a greater chance to unite your willingness and desire with the effective outcome.

The human in survival mode is ingrained to be 'doing' and so we gift you with another option: Allow this life, this entire cosmic experience to be God's demonstration to you of what is possible! And so it is!

Often it is hard to discern when one is surrendered and when one is not. How do we know if we are surrendered to the Divine Grace of God and it is moving through Me or it is 'me'?

The union of 'You and Me' is fully complete but in the way of a three legged race, where a team is tied together at the ankle, and either partner may affect the direction of the team. And so what is requested is that your focus be upon the Higher Self, the Guidance, the unpremeditated subtle movements—these are the Divine in action. In the absence of strong ideas of where to go and how to do things, emptiness brings Grace. And so the empty presence, the now moment, the willing heart attuned to the Divine directive and impulse, allows Divinity access to your life. So, all aspects of

The empty presence, the now moment, the willing heart attuned to the Divine directive and impulse, allows Divinity access to your life.

this relationship are invisible until they aren't.

And so, proactively focus upon the relationship with the Higher Self as 'me' within the willing emptiness to the answer you 'seek.' It is really an end to the 'seeking' that is the ultimate answer. That is something that is worth noting here in surrendering to the equality of each and every moment, where a moment on the beach in Bermuda is of the same value as a moment in the rain being splashed by life—that is the equanimity of the human while allowing, guided and surrendering to LIFE ITSELF—the One Life. A true God in action is different than in the human in that everything is SELF. And so from God's perspective, to judge the beach or the rain doesn't make any sense. It is only from the human's physicality that this (judging) occurs and re-occurs. And so this chance now is to surrender in final release from that judging and allow the grace of the Divine impulse to flow in and through you, by your focus upon that relationship and the empty presence you offer to it.

So you are saying that we can't know this by a particular outcome that occurs, we can only know this by leaning into the relationship?

Yes, this is true at one level. Yet if there is a result like a door that opens of its own accord, you will have a clue that it is not solely of your human will that this occurs! In that same vein, the realization that 'You Are That, You Are Divine Will' and also that 'You are the human in form'—this fusion of both opportunities into one LIFE that lives by your attention and a grace in allowing it, that is what is occurring in a Life lead by Love. And so it is.

Surrender was recently clarified for me when Jesus said *'For now, the real message is surrender to the One. Not surrender in the sense of being un-attuned to direction, but in being aligned to Truth. That is the delineation that is worth noting here. To align to Truth, this means to be centrally focused at all times.'*

Leaning Into Love Exercise: Stop for a moment and lean into loving your Higher Self, the Life that flows through all. Make a commitment to your Higher Self to be centrally focused and to listen for its promptings, inspiration and guidance.

Relationships: Loving God In Human Form
I realized that the reason why it can be hard to be on a path of spiritual surrender, while in relationship with another person is that the subtle 'leaning in to Divine will' and being centrally focused is redirected towards leaning outward to the relationship with another person. Thus, leading a person to be on a path to union with a human, not a Union with God.

Sai Maa encourages celibacy and a single life for some and I can understand why in the light of this. That leaning into God, leaning into Love and the inner focus is subtle and it is easy to be pulled out of it without realizing it. For me, the results of doing so can include that end of the day awareness that I haven't fed some part of my greater Self's existence or work. Although it is also a joy to love another, to love one's children, family and friends in devotion to whatever is called for in those relationships. Do you have any comment on this Jesus?

Dear One, the path does not judge the path of the ONE LIFE as it lives itself through the human family. It is equally content in the lowliest or the grandest expression. What IS different from one life to the next, is it's measure of human will vs. God's will within it and in the amount of Love that is expressed, either in relationship, in being single or in a crowd. It is simply that. No need to wonder if you are in God's hands, if you are Loving, if you are in Love, if you are Love, there should be no doubt. So it is not the outer circumstances of a life that are indicative of its value in this regard, it is the inner quotient of Love. Love of Self, Love of other, Love of Life and Love of God. And so it is.

No need to wonder if you are in God's hands, if you are Loving, if you are in Love, if you are Love, there should be no doubt.

Thank you that was so helpful. So it sounds like the answer to 'My life? God's life?'... is that it's Love's Life!

16. SURRENDER TO LIFE, COMPLETE IN THE ONE

Dear Reader, knowing what you do of the world, of the challenges and the opportunities of human existence, we invite your reflection upon the way that this New World might be brought into our experience as a collective society, as a Family of Man and Woman. It need not be a difficult task. It needs only your wholehearted and engaged participation, thus filling you with the Truth and Love that you seek in Life. It is always a small part of humanity that at first makes significant changes in the face of environmental pressure and societal need. You Dear One, are of that band of Life. You, responding to the call of your inner voice, are right here now. Even as these words are written, you are ready for this next stage in human evolution to Light.

The time ahead is one where the Human form will be a supporting structure for the One Life that flows through all. It holds the species dearly poised for a grand elevation of potential in freedom and joyful union with Life. As the blessed wisdom of the higher aspects of yourself come into Life's journey on Earth, there is a chance to be a leader, to create Heaven on Earth in the Golden

Age of Light. It means letting go of old ways and structures that no longer serve. And so, as you are the vessel for this New World, awake, aware and willing to participate in Life fully, there is a miracle that occurs both in your own life and in the lives of those you touch. Freedom exists within relationships with each other, within our Love of Life and the process we are in formation with. Love the process and all else will be revealed.

My wish for you is that these pages have enriched your capacity for this kind of transformation in your life. That you leave our time together in this book a larger being, a greater Love, an embodied God as Human. This is your path; this is what you have come to Earth to perform. There is nothing else on Earth that will satisfy you as this does. It is beyond measure in its value for Life.

Not knowing how this might occur is no impediment to its occurring! Remember this… have faith. Think ye not that this is a job beyond divine brilliance to reform it, to reform a society? Or, to uplift a species awake and willing, to new levels of demonstration and Life? Nothing is beyond the capacities of a Human species grounded in Love. Everyone is a part of such opportunity.

The realization that 'All That Is,' is already present within you is a glimpse into the potential of Life. If everything that has been made and that is in the world of created Life is already present within 'me,' how can I need for anything or anyone? It is that surety and completeness that will be the platform of this Higher potential, not grounded in lack or need or want, but grounded in Love, surety, conviction of God's 'unwavering Truth of Unity of All' and malice towards none. This final line is worth noting. In malice towards nothing, inside of you or outside of you, you will note that you are Whole. You are Home, you are One. That is the final marker and arbiter of your freedom.

Congratulations for making it this far to this revealing of Life's Truth in words pointing towards your Heart. Your Home awaits, be present in it as the door swings open and as the world around you awaits your free associations that will share it so beautifully with the rest. This is the time we have all waited for and You are the path that will take us there. Behold your True Nature in the Life you lead. Allow it expression, allow its fusion with the very core of Life and this will be the way Home for You.

Not wishing to end this book in a way that is not conclusive for You, please consider your part in assimilation and practice of these messages of Light. Your work is to meet your Higher Self halfway up the mountain. Our work together is to reach the peak. Do not fear that it is not possible, simply realize that it is hard to fall up to the top. It requires the 'work' of one step after the other. The thing that will ensure the destination of the peak and not a circling of the summit, is the awareness of your Godhood and the possibility of Miracles that exist within your very own Heart and Hands.

You are embodied Love in Life. You are the only way for information that comes through you to be dispersed. You are affecting the world you touch right here and remotely as well. And so be strong in your conviction that 'all is well.' Reside in the perfection 'That Is.' Know that You are Truth, Love and Oneness as you surrender to the Light within You and as you allow the grace of God to infuse your being. Making space for your Higher Self, You discover who You truly are.

Namaste we are One and so it is.

Upon the mountaintop we reside in Holy Communion and Light, recognize that this mountaintop and the Light are yours already and our task is complete!

The End

GLOSSARY

Christ: *"means God-Principle flowing through the individual."*[32] In *Be The Second Coming* I asked "What is the full manifestation of Christ Consciousness?"

And Jesus said: *"The Christed Self indwelling and eternal as it exists in manifest expression through the living human form, not only as a human being, but as a God incarnate —as the potential lies in all incarnated humans. It is really quite simply an expression of one who has allowed the Truth of 'what is' to express itself fully in form, without interference or distortion on the level of the human. Namaste. We are One."*[33]

Deva: *The energy intelligences that assist matter into the physical forms of life.*[34]

Devic Realm: "parallel to the human realm and is a kingdom that is hierarchal, including elementals, fairies, gnomes, water and garden sprites, nature spirits and devas of various levels.

---

32 Spalding, Baird T. *Life and Teaching of the Masters of the Far East,* Marina del Ray, CA, 1935.
33 Mauran, Hope Ives. *Be The Second Coming,* Bloomington, IN, Balboa Press, 2011. (pg. 54)
34 Stodola, Michael. Author of handout on devas, he does energy clearings in cooperation with the devic realm. http://www. ablecrystals.com/contact.html

There now are also devic energies reflecting our electronic and technical creations."[35]

God: "God is."[36] All That Is, Source, the One.

Higher Self, Christed Self: Our Higher Octave or Higher Frequency Divine Impersonal Self.

human self: (lowercase) The perspective from which most of us have lived our lives until now, where we believe ourselves separate from everything else and 'only human.'

Jesus: (In his own words.) *Envision human potential at its highest opportunity for Life, this is what the present day Jesus now embodies, no longer tied to a human flesh and blood form, but fluidly coming and going as needed and desired. Yet while too, taking on higher responsibilities and works around the evolution and upliftment of the human species. So much grace has come of this transition, and so much is asked of those who face this choice now.*

Miracle: The actual Truth revealing itself. The expression of the 'One' touching the illusionary human world and thus revealing the true state of Unity.

Self: capitalized means the individual in Oneness, Divinity or Christ Consciousness.

---

35 Ibid.
36 Reynard, Gary. *The Disappearance of The Universe.*

BIBLIOGRAPHY

Calleman, Carl Johan. *The Mayan Calendar and the Transformation of Consciousness*. Rochester, VT, Bear & Company, 2004.

Cota-Robles, Patricia Diane. *Divine Alchemy,* Tucson, AZ, New Age Study of Humanity's Purpose, CD, 2012.

Gautschi, Paul. *Back To Eden*. (DVD)

Grace, Raymon. *Raymon Grace Energizes Water II*. (DVD)

Grace, Raymon. *http://www.raymongraceprojects.com,* December 2012 Online Newsletter.

Green, Glenda. *Love Without End, Jesus Speaks,* Sedona, AZ, Spiritis,1999.

Hrehorczak-Stephens, Tamara. *Abraham Kawai'I, A brief history of the man, the kahuna, and kahuna bodywork,* Tamara Hrehorczak-Stephens, 2012.

Lipton, Bruce H. and Bhaerman, Steve. *Spontaneous Evolution, Our Positive Future (And A Way To Get There From Here)*, Carlsbad, CA, Hay House, 2009.

Mauran, Hope Ives. *Be The Second Coming, Guidebook To The Embodiment Of The Christ Within, A personal Journey, Our Collective Destiny,* Bloomington, IN, Balboa Press, 2011.

McTaggart, Lynne. *The Field: The Quest for the Secret Force of the Universe,* New York, Harper Collins, 2002.

Renard, Gary R. *The Disappearance of the Universe: Straight Talk About Illusions, Past Lives, Religion, Sex, Politics, and the Miracles of Forgiveness,* Carlsbad, CA, Hay House, Inc., 2002.

Spalding, Baird T. *Life and Teaching of the Masters of the Far East.* 6 vols. Marina del Rey, CA, DeVorss, 1972.

Scott, Steven K. *The Greatest Words Ever Spoken,* Colorado Springs, WaterBrook, 2008.

Wolf, Stefan. *Ecovillages and Self-reliant communities in Europe,* Stateline, NV, Ringing Cedars Press, 2010. (DVD)

Yogananda, Paramahansa. *The Second Coming of Christ. Vol. 1 of The Resurrection of the Christ Within You.* Los Angeles, CA, Self-Realization Fellowship, 2004.

ABOUT THE 'AUTHOR'

HOPE IVES MAURAN has been blessed to be a student of many voices for the One, some of whom are listed here: Ibrahim Karim's Biogeometry, Kahu Abraham Kawai'I, Harry Uhane Jim, Sadhguru Jaggi Vasudev's Isha Yoga, Ariel Spilsbury, Craig Hamilton and Sai Maa Lakshmi Devi.

"Thank you for reading this book, please share it with your friends."

Photo Credit: Maggie Heinzel-Neel

As an inter-dimensional translator, Hope has written *Be The Second Coming, Guidebook To The Embodiment Of The Christ Within, A Personal Journey, Our Collective Destiny,* (2011) and *Where the Wisdom Lies: A Message from Nature's Small Creatures,* (2006). She also wrote and recorded a teaching CD entitled *Emotional Transformation: Learn to Speak the Language of Creation.*[37] As an artist, Hope creates eco-spiritual modified landscapes, guided drawings and illustrations of the spiritual journey.[38]

---

37 Available for free on her website www.hopeivesmauran.com
38 Available in the offerings part of www.hopeivesmauran.com is the mind map called "what if" which is free to download. The artwork may be viewed on the website too.

CPSIA information can be obtained at www.ICGtesting.com
Printed in the USA
BVOW07s1220091113

335810BV00003B/8/P